Dear Reader,

Hanukkah celebrates a great victory for religious freedom—the triumph of a few over many, of a small band of Jews over a mighty army. It also celebrates the miracle of a small cruse of oil that burned and burned. Collected in this book, along with the history, laws, and customs of Hanukkah, are recipes, stories, music, riddles, magic, and games. It is a fact-filled, fun-filled book, one you'll come back to year after year.

This book was a joy to compile, and as I worked on it, I celebrated Hanukkah almost daily, month after month. I hope you find joy in it, too, and that it enhances your delight with our great winter holiday.

David A. Adler

The Kids' Catalog of
Hanukkah

This book is lovingly dedicated to
our dear grandchildren

Elias, Ethan, and Hannelora

by their grandpa and grandma

Henry (ז"ל) and Edith Everett

The Kids' Catalog of
Hanukkah

David A. Adler

The Jewish Publication Society
Philadelphia
2004 • 5764

Contributing Editors	Hanna Yerushalmi
	Janice Cane
Production Editor	Janet L. Liss
Production Manager	Robin Norman
Recipe Consultant	Anita Hirsch
Editorial Assistant	Miri Pomerantz
Illustrations	David A. Adler and Avi Katz
Design/Composition	Eliz. Anne O'Donnell

The Jewish Publication Society
2100 Arch Street
Philadelphia, PA 19103

Manufactured in the United States of America
04 05 06 07 08 09 10 10 9 8 7 6 5 4 3 2 1

Library of Congress Cataloging-in-Publication Data

Adler, David A.
  The kids' catalog of Hanukkah / David A. Adler.-- 1st ed.
     v. cm.
  Includes index.
  Contents: All about Hanukkah -- Hanukkah stories -- Hanukkah fun.
  ISBN 0-8276-0805-5 (alk. paper)
  1. Hanukkah--Juvenile literature. [1. Hanukkah.] I. Title.
  BM695.H3A652 2004
  296.4'35--dc22
                                        2003027949

All recommendations and suggestions for recipes and crafts are made without any guarantees on the part of the author or The Jewish Publication Society. Because of differing tools, materials, conditions, and individual skills, the author and publisher disclaim liability for any injuries, losses, or other damages that may result from using the information in this book.

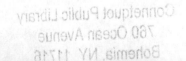

Contents

PART ONE
All About Hanukkah

Hanukkah Mazes

Games

Magic

Puzzle Fun

Notes from the Publisher

A safety note about the crafts in this book:

Some of the crafts in this book call for the use of scissors or other potentially dangerous tools. Before beginning any craft, get either help or the "go-ahead" from a responsible adult. Read the directions and assemble all the materials you will need before you begin.

This recipe involves sharp knives and a hot pan.

Ask an adult for help.

A safety note about the recipes in this book:

A kitchen can be a dangerous place. Watch out for splattering oil or boiling water. Some of the recipes in this book are intended only for older children. Before beginning any of the recipes, make sure an adult is available to help. Read the entire recipe and assemble all the ingredients and utensils (pots, pans, spoons, knives, and so forth) before you begin.

This recipe involves hot oil that can splatter and burn.

Ask an adult for help.

A note about the spellings in this book:

There are many ways to spell Hebrew words using the English alphabet. *Hanukkah*, for example, is frequently spelled *Chanukah*, and *dreidel* is often spelled *dreydl*. Some of the stories and music in this book contained different spellings when they were originally published. Whenever possible, we have been faithful to the spelling used in the original publications.

The Story of Hanukkah

by DAVID A. ADLER

The story of Hanukkah begins in Israel long ago. The country was called Judea then, and the Jews who lived there did not rule their land. Different kings with their armies marched through Judea. First one ruled the land, then another. But while Judea was ruled by different kings, the Jews lived there as they always had. The farmers planted and harvested. The shepherds watched their sheep. And on holidays they all went up to the Temple in Jerusalem.

The Temple was beautiful. It stood on top of a mountain. Inside were gold crowns and gates covered with gold and silver. There was a *ner tamid*, a light that always burned, and a gold vine with gold leaves and grapes hanging from it. No iron was used in building the Temple. That's because iron is a tool of war, and the Temple was a place of peace. It was called "The House of God."

There were no idols in the Temple. Other people worshiped many gods. They prayed and bowed to idols. But the Jews, led by the high priest, prayed to just one god, the God who created the heaven and earth.

The Jews kept their holidays. They lived in peace until a Greek, Antiochus the Fourth, ruled Judea.

It was not enough for Antiochus that his people paid him high taxes. He wanted them all to take Greek names, read Greek books, and play Greek sports.

Antiochus forced the Jews to take a new high priest, named Menelaus. Soon, he began stealing gold and silver from the Temple and sending it to Antiochus.

The Jews hated the new high priest. While Antiochus was fighting a war in Egypt, a small army of Jewish soldiers surrounded the Temple. They forced Menelaus out.

But then Antiochus returned. His army was with him. He saw the soldiers in Jerusalem and thought the Jews were rising up against him. With his army, he stormed the city. They tore down the city walls. It was the Sabbath. The Jews wouldn't fight back and

All About Hanukkah

thousands were killed. Homes were burned. Women and children were carried off and sold as slaves.

Antiochus and his men marched into the Temple. They marched out with everything they could carry. Later a Greek idol was placed in the Temple. Any Jew who refused to bow and sacrifice an animal to the idol was killed. So were Jews who lit Sabbath candles or studied Jewish law.

The king's soldiers went throughout Judea and forced the Jews to bow and worship Greek idols. Some Jews obeyed the king. Many others didn't and were killed.

Then the king's men came to the town of Modin. They set up their idol and asked an old priest named Mattathias to worship it. Mattathias refused. But another man was frightened and was ready to worship the idol. Mattathias rushed forward. He struck the man and one of the soldiers. He threw down the idol and called out, "Whoever is for the Lord our God, follow me!" And he ran off into the hills. His five sons and many other Jews followed him.

Antiochus heard what happened in Modin. He sent an army after Mattathias and his followers. But each time the soldiers came near, the rocks and caves seemed to open up. Brave Jews attacked the strong army of Antiochus. Then they ran back to the hills and hid.

One army general remembered that the Jews would not fight on the Sabbath, so that's when he attacked. Many Jews were killed until Mattathias told his men that they must fight back, even on the Sabbath.

The Jews were farmers and shepherds. But they fought like brave soldiers. First they fought under Mattathias. Then, when Mattathias died, his son Judah became their leader. Judah was called the Maccabee, the hammer. The people who fought with him were called Maccabees.

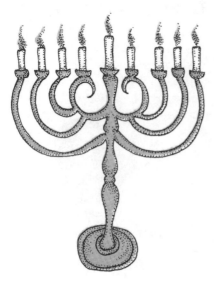

Antiochus sent his best generals with large armies to fight the Maccabees. The armies came with bows, arrows, swords, horses, and armored elephants. For one battle, slave traders even came along leading empty wagons. After the battle, the traders planned to capture the beaten, frightened Maccabees and sell them as slaves.

It never happened.

The Maccabees surprised the armies of Antiochus. Once, the Maccabees caught them in a narrow pass between two mountains. From the tops and sides of the mountains, it was easy for the Maccabees to fight their enemies down below.

Another time, Judah knew that the soldiers of Antiochus were ready to attack. He lit a ring of campfires and led his men away. Then, while half the enemy's army was attacking the empty campsite, Judah and the Maccabees surprised the other half.

In the final battle, there were more than six of the enemy for each Maccabee. But still, the mighty army of Antiochus was beaten. And Judah led the Maccabees to Jerusalem.

The Temple in Jerusalem was overgrown with thorns and weeds. It was filled with garbage. When the Maccabees first saw it,

The Holiday of Hanukkah

We light candles in our homes on each of the eight nights of Hanukkah. And, as the candles burn, we sing about the Hanukkah miracles.

We eat latkes, potato pancakes fried in oil. And we play a game with a square spinning top, a dreidel. On each of the four sides of the dreidel is a different Hebrew letter. They are the first four letters of the Hebrew sentence, *nes gadol haya shami*, which means, "A great miracle happened there."

In many homes children are given gifts and Hanukkah gelt. Hanukkah gelt is Hanukkah money, and it is often used in the dreidel games. The gifts are just an added way to make the holiday a happy one.

The candles, the songs, the oil in the latkes, and the letters of the dreidel remind us of the miracles that happened during the time of Judah and his father, Mattathias. The miracles, of course, are the small jar of oil that burned for so long and the small group of Maccabees who fought a mighty king and won.

Ever since that first Hanukkah, Jews just like the Maccabees have fought for the right to pray to God and live as Jews. And today, in certain parts of the world, Jews are still fighting for the very same things.

they cried. They tore their clothes and mourned. Then they worked to clean the Temple. They built a new altar, new gates, and new doors.

When it came time to light the *ner tamid*, the Maccabees searched for oil. They found just one small jar, enough to burn for only one day. But the oil in that small jar burned and burned until more oil could be prepared. The oil that was enough for one day burned for eight days, and the *ner tamid* did not go out.

On the twenty-fifth day of the Hebrew month of Kislev, the Temple became again the "House of God." The Jews celebrated. They prayed and sang for eight days. Then Judah declared that every year, on the twenty-fifth of Kislev, an eight-day holiday would begin. The holiday was called Hanukkah, which means dedication. It celebrates the day the Temple was rededicated to God.

That was over two thousand years ago. But today, all over the world, Jews still celebrate Hanukkah.

Why You Won't Find Hanukkah in the Bible

Hanukkah, also called "The Feast of Dedication" and "The Feast of the Maccabees" is the only Jewish festival that is not mentioned in the Bible. Why is this? Because the holiday of Hanukkah is too young! Even though we have been celebrating Hanukkah for over two thousand years—since 165 B.C.E—Jewish history goes back so far in time that even something that happened two thousand years ago is still a "recent" event. Hanukkah is so new, compared to stories like the Exodus from Egypt, that the Bible had already been written by the time Judah Maccabee led the revolt against the Greeks.

The story of the Maccabees is told in the four Books of the Maccabees, which are found in a collection of writings called the Apocrypha. Also, there are passages in the Book of Daniel, in the third section of the Bible, Ketuvim (Writings), that contain a foreshadowing of the Hanukkah revolt. In this book, the prophet Daniel, who lived four hundred years before the Maccabees, has a dream that seems to predict events that are very similar to those of the Hanukkah story.

Hanukkah the Name

by CHAIM BERGER

In Hebrew, the word "Hanukkah" means "dedication." That would, of course, refer to the Maccabees' rededication, or reconsecration, of the Temple after their victory over the Syrian Greeks. Other commentators point out also, though, that the word is a combination of *"hanu,"* which means rested, and *"kah,"* a combination of the Hebrew letters *kaf* and *hey*, which has the numerical value of twenty-five. This indicates that the Maccabees rested (from fighting) on the *kah*, the twenty-fifth (of Kislev).

If you take the first letters of each of the words of the following sentence—*"Het nerot ve'halaha ke'Bet Hillel"*—you have the word

Why Celebrate Eight Days of Hanukkah?

According to the Talmud, when the Jews tried to rededicate the Temple by lighting the *ner tamid*, the eternal light, there was only enough pure oil to burn for one night. We celebrate the miracle that the oil lasted for seven extra days. Why, then, do we celebrate an eight-day holiday and not a seven-day one?

One answer is that there were really two miracles. The first miracle was that there was one jar of oil that the Greeks didn't destroy. The second was that this small vessel of oil lasted seven days longer than everyone expected. So we celebrate one day for the first miracle, and the next seven for the second miracle.

Another answer is that the first day of Hanukkah celebrates the victory of the Maccabees over the powerful army of Antiochus IV, and the rest of the days of Hanukkah celebrate the miracle of the oil.

"*Hanukkah.*" The sentence means "Eight candles and the rule is like the School of Hillel." The last part refers to the fact that we light one candle the first night and we increase the number by one each night until we have eight the last night.

BLESSING

The Blessings on Lighting Hanukkah Candles

The primary Hanukkah ritual is the kindling, the lighting, of the lights. This is performed soon after nightfall. On Friday it precedes the kindling of the Shabbat candles.

The *shammash* candle is lit and used to kindle the others. One, set in the extreme right candleholder, is lit on the first night of Hanukkah. On each succeeding night another candle is added to the left until all eight candles are lit on the eighth night. The kindling is from left to right. The same procedure is followed if oil and wicks are used.

The following two blessings are chanted each night before kindling the lights:

בָּרוּךְ אַתָּה יְיָ אֱלֹהֵינוּ מֶלֶךְ הָעוֹלָם, אֲשֶׁר קִדְּשָׁנוּ

בְּמִצְוֹתָיו וְצִוָּנוּ לְהַדְלִיק נֵר שֶׁל חֲנוּכָּה.

בָּרוּךְ אַתָּה יְיָ אֱלֹהֵינוּ מֶלֶךְ הָעוֹלָם, שֶׁעָשָׂה נִסִּים לַאֲבוֹתֵינוּ בַּיָּמִים הָהֵם בַּזְּמַן הַזֶּה.

Baruch Ata Adonai, Eloheinu Melekh ha-olam, asher kideshanu bemitzvotav vetzivanu lehadlik ner shel Hanukkah.

Baruch Ata Adonai, Eloheinu Melech ha-olam, she-asa nissim la-avotenu, bayamim hahem, bazman hazeh.

"Blessed are You, Lord our God, Ruler of the universe, who has sancti-fied us with Your commandments and has commanded us to kindle the Hanukkah lights."

"Blessed are You, Lord our God, Ruler of the universe, who performed miracles for our fathers in those days, at this season."

The following blessing is chanted only on the first night of Hanukkah:

בָּרוּךְ אַתָּה יְיָ אֱלֹהֵינוּ מֶלֶךְ הָעוֹלָם, שֶׁהֶחֱיָנוּ וְקִיְּמָנוּ וְהִגִּיעָנוּ לַזְּמַן הַזֶּה.

Baruch Ata Adonai, Eloheinu Melech ha-olam, shehecheyanu, ve-kiye-manu, ve-higi-anu lazman hazeh.

"Blessed are You, Lord our God, Ruler of the universe, who has granted us life, sustained us, and brought us to this season."

After kindling the first light, the following passage is read or chanted:

BLESSING
Hanerot Hallalu (These Lights)

הַנֵּרוֹת הַלָּלוּ אֲנַחְנוּ מַדְלִיקִים עַל הַנִּסִּים וְעַל הַנִּפְלָאוֹת וְעַל הַתְּשׁוּעוֹת וְעַל הַמִּלְחָמוֹת שֶׁעָשִׂיתָ לַאֲבוֹתֵינוּ בַּיָּמִים הָהֵם, בַּזְּמַן הַזֶּה, עַל יְדֵי כֹּהֲנֶיךָ הַקְּדוֹשִׁים. וְכָל שְׁמוֹנַת יְמֵי חֲנוּכָּה, הַנֵּרוֹת הַלָּלוּ קֹדֶשׁ הֵם וְאֵין לָנוּ רְשׁוּת לְהִשְׁתַּמֵּשׁ בָּהֶם אֶלָּא לִרְאוֹתָם בִּלְבָד, כְּדֵי לְהוֹדוֹת וּלְהַלֵּל לְשִׁמְךָ הַגָּדוֹל עַל נִסֶּיךָ וְעַל יְשׁוּעָתֶךָ וְעַל נִפְלְאוֹתֶיךָ.

Hanerot hallalu anachnu madlikim al ha-nissim, ve-al ha-niflaot, ve-al ha-teshuot, ve-al ha-milchamot she-asita la-avotenu bayamim hahem bazman hazeh, al yedei kohanecha ha-kedoshim. Ve-chol shemonat yemai Hanuk-kah, hanerot hallalu, kodesh hem, ve-ain lanu reshut le-hishtamesh ba-hem, ela lirotam bil-vad, kedai lehodot u-le-hallel lish-mecha ha-gadol, al nisecha, ve-al yeshu-otecha, ve-al nifle-otecha.

"We kindle these lights to honor the miracles, wonders, rescues, and victorious battles You granted our fathers in those days, at this season, through Your holy priests. During all the eight days of Hanukkah these lights are sacred, and we are not permitted to make use of them. Rather, we are only to look at them in order to give thanks and to praise Your great name, for Your miracles, Your wonders, and Your salvations.

BLESSING
Al ha-Nissim
(For the Miracles)

In the Grace after Meals (Birkat ha-Mazon) as well as in the Amidah (the Eighteen Benedictions, said silently while standing), an additional prayer is recited throughout the eight days of Hanukkah. Al ha-Nissim is a song of thanksgiving and praise for divine intervention and deliverance from the enemy (its title means "For the Miracles"). Epitomizing the Maccabean struggle, it emphasizes the spiritual over the military aspect. While an abbreviated text of Al ha-Nissim is in the Talmud, the current version is first found in the prayer book of Rav Amram Gaon, head of the academy in Sura, Babylonia, in the ninth century.

עַל הַנִּסִּים וְעַל הַפֻּרְקָן וְעַל הַגְּבוּרוֹת וְעַל הַתְּשׁוּעוֹת

וְעַל הַמִּלְחָמוֹת שֶׁעָשִׂיתָ לַאֲבוֹתֵינוּ בַּיָּמִים הָהֵם וּבַזְּמַן הַזֶּה.

בִּימֵי מַתִּתְיָהוּ בֶּן-יוֹחָנָן [כֹּהֵן גָּדוֹל] חַשְׁמוֹנַאי וּבָנָיו כְּשֶׁעָמְדָה

מַלְכוּת יָוָן הָרְשָׁעָה עַל עַמְּךָ יִשְׂרָאֵל לְהַשְׁכִּיחָם תּוֹרָתֶךָ

וּלְהַעֲבִירָם מֵחֻקֵּי רְצוֹנֶךָ. וְאַתָּה בְּרַחֲמֶיךָ הָרַבִּים עָמַדְתָּ לָהֶם

בְּעֵת צָרָתָם רַבְתָּ אֶת-רִיבָם, דַּנְתָּ אֶת-דִּינָם, נָקַמְתָּ אֶת-
נִקְמָתָם, מָסַרְתָּ גִּבּוֹרִים בְּיַד חַלָּשִׁים, וְרַבִּים בְּיַד מְעַטִּים,
וּטְמֵאִים בְּיַד טְהוֹרִים, וּרְשָׁעִים בְּיַד צַדִּיקִים, וְזֵדִים בְּיַד
עוֹסְקֵי תוֹרָתֶךָ. וּלְךָ עָשִׂיתָ שֵׁם גָּדוֹל וְקָדוֹשׁ בְּעוֹלָמֶךָ, וּלְעַמְּךָ
יִשְׂרָאֵל עָשִׂיתָ תְּשׁוּעָה גְדוֹלָה וּפֻרְקָן כְּהַיּוֹם הַזֶּה. וְאַחַר כֵּן בָּאוּ
בָנֶיךָ לִדְבִיר בֵּיתֶךָ וּפִנּוּ אֶת-הֵיכָלֶךָ וְטִהֲרוּ אֶת-מִקְדָּשֶׁךָ,
וְהִדְלִיקוּ נֵרוֹת בְּחַצְרוֹת קָדְשֶׁךָ וְקָבְעוּ שְׁמוֹנַת יְמֵי חֲנֻכָּה אֵלּוּ,
לְהוֹדוֹת וּלְהַלֵּל לְשִׁמְךָ הַגָּדוֹל.

Al ha-nissim ve-al ha-purkan, ve-al ha-gevurot, ve-al ha-teshuot ve-al ha-milchamot she-asita la-avotenu bayamim hahem bazman hazeh. Be-yemei Matityahu ben Yochanan [kohen gadol] Hashmonai u-vanav ke-she-amdah malchut Yavan harsha-a al amcha Yisrael le-hashkicham Torahtecha u-le-ha-aviram mechukei retzonecha. Ve-ata be-rachamecha harabim amadeta lahem be-et tzaratam ravta et-rivam, danta et-dinam, nakamta et-nikmatam, masarta giborim be-yad chalashim, ve-rabim be-yad mi-atim, u-timei-im be-yad tihorim, u-rasha-im be-yad tzadikim, ve-zeidim be-yad oskei Torahtecha. U-lecha asita shem gadol ve-kadosh be-olamecha, u-le-amcha Yisrael asita teshua gedola u-furkan ke-hayom hazeh. Ve-achar ken ba-u vanecha lidvir beitecha u-finu et-heichalecha ve-tiharu et-mikdashecha, ve-hidliku nerot be-chatzrot kadshecha ve-kavu shmonat yemei Hanukkah eilu, lehodot u-le-hallel lishmecha ha-gadol.

We thank You for the miracles, triumphs, heroism, rescues, and battles that You waged for our fathers in those days at this time. In the days of Mattathias, son of Johanan the Hasmonean high priest, and his sons, the kingdom of the evil Greeks arose against the people of Israel and demanded that the Jews abandon Your Torah and violate Your mitzvot. And You, God, in Your great mercy, stood by them in their hour of need. You fought for them, defended them, and avenged their wrongs. You delivered the strong into the hands of the weak, the many into the hands of the few, the corrupt into the hands of the pure, the guilty into the hands of the innocent, and the arrogant into the hands of those faithful to Your Torah.

Thus, You achieved a great and holy name in the world and You brought a great redemption and liberation to Your people Israel to this day. Afterward Your children reentered the Holy of Holies, Your Temple, to clean Your sanctuary, to purify Your altar, and to kindle lights in Your sacred courts. And they set aside these eight days of Hanukkah to give thanks and to praise Your great name.

SONG

"Maoz Tzur" (Rock of Ages): A Closer Look at the Song

"Maoz Tzur" (Rock of Ages) is one of the most popular hymns sung by Ashkenazic Jews, those who come from central and eastern Europe. It is generally accepted that it was written in the 13th century by someone named Mordecai.

The song praises God for redeeming Israel from Egyptian slavery (recalled especially at Passover) and from the Babylonian exile, for saving the Persian Jews from the evil Haman's plot to exterminate the Jews (celebrated more specifically on Purim), and for helping the Jews triumph over Antiochus IV Epiphanes (remembered during Hanukkah). Finally, the song expresses the hope that those nations guilty of persecuting Jews in modern times will be avenged and Israel will be redeemed from exile.

The origin of the melody is a medieval German folk song; however, the stirring tune underwent changes over the course of time. The English version written by Solomon Solis-Cohen is a free translation that attempts to adhere to the rhyme scheme and spirit of the original Hebrew while retaining the basic ideas of the song.

"Rock of Ages"
translated by SOLOMON SOLIS-COHEN

> *Mighty, praised beyond compare,*
> *Rock of my salvation,*
> *Build again my house of prayer,*
> *For Thy habitation!*
> *Offering and libation, shall a ransomed nation*
> *Joyful bring*
> *There, and sing*
> *Psalms of dedication!*
>
> *Woe was mine in Egypt-land,*
> *(Tyrant kings enslaved me):*

Why was Illana spinning around the room?

She forgot to let go of the dreidel.

Till Thy mighty outstretched hand
From oppression saved me.
Pharaoh, rash pursuing, vowed my swift undoing;
Soon his host
That proud boast
'Neath the waves was ruling!

To Thy holy hill, the way
Madest Thou clear before me;
With false gods I went astray—
Foes to exile bore me.
Torn from all I cherished, almost had I perished;
Babylon fell,
Ze-rub-ba-bel
Badest Thou restore me!

Then the vengeful Haman wrought
Subtly, to betray me;
In his snare himself he caught—
He that plann'd to slay me.
(Hailed from Esther's palace; hanged on his own gallows!)
Seal and ring
Persia's king
Gave Thy servant zealous.

When the brave Asmonéans broke
Javan's chain in sunder,
Through the holy oil Thy folk
Didst Thou show a wonder.
Ever full remainèd the vessel unprofanèd;
These eight days.
Light and praise,
There were ordained.

Lord, Thy holy arm make bare,
Speed my restoration;
Be my martyr's blood Thy care—
Judge each guilty nation.
Long is my probation; sore my tribulation—
Bid, from heaven,
Thy shepherds seven
Haste to my salvation!

Oil is the Key Ingredient!

According to the Talmud, oil played a key role in the rededication of the Temple. The Maccabees defeated the Greeks, and their first job was to take the Temple back. The Jews were so excited! They all gathered in the Temple and waited for the high priest to relight the menorah. The only thing they needed was some uncontaminated oil. They looked around for some but couldn't find any; the Greek soldiers had smashed all of the oil jugs.

Or so they thought!

Hidden in a dark corner was a small jar of oil. The high priest was glad to see it, but such a little bit! He poured it into the menorah and hoped for the best. The people rejoiced to see light, which meant that the Temple belonged once again to the Jews. They celebrated all day long. Then, as the day ended, they looked at the menorah in fear, worried that it would go out. But, the oil kept burning and burning. For eight

days it burned—and this is the miracle of Hanukkah.

Today the production of olive oil is a big industry in Israel. You can find olive trees throughout the country. In some places the trees are one to two thousand years old! During harvest time, the trees are full of olives. Ripe olives are usually green, just about to turn black. And it is then that they are ready to be pressed, in order to release their oil. The first oil that comes from the pressing is called "virgin" olive oil and is used for special purposes. In the Bible it is used to anoint kings and to prepare sacrifices. The Jews used it to light the Temple menorah.

Today olives are a nutritious and regular part of the Israeli diet, and many items crafted in Israel, such as wooden dreidels and menorahs, are made from olive wood.

The Order for Candle Lighting

The numbers on top of the candles is the order they should be placed in the menorah. The number alongside the candles is the order in which they should be lit.

First night

Second night

Third night

Fourth night

Fifth night

Sixth night

Seventh night

Eighth night

The Laws of Hanukkah

Although Hanukkah seems like a easy holiday to celebrate, there are many questions about the practice of the holiday that can arise, such as: where and when to light the candles, who should light them, and what should be done on the Sabbath. In an effort to answer some of these questions, a list of Hanukkah rules were created. The following traditional guidelines have been adapted from "The Law of Israel," taken from *The Hayye Adam* (The Life of Man), compiled and arranged by Rabbi Bernard Abramowitz and translated by V. Samuel David Aaronson.

Although we may not follow many of these rules in our own homes, they highlight the importance of this joyous celebration:

1. On the twenty-fifth day of the Hebrew month of Kislev (which usually falls during the months of November or December), the eight days of Hanukkah begin. Every night, lights are lit near doors or windows of homes to publicize the Hanukkah miracle. During the holiday, it is important to talk about the Hanukkah miracles. Hanukkah meals should be somewhat more lavish than usual meals, and it is customary to eat dairy foods. On Hanukkah, charity should be given generously.

2. Both men and women should light Hanukkah candles, and a woman may light the candles for her family. A blind person should contribute something toward the purchase of candles that will be lit by someone else.

3. A *shammash* or lighting candle is lit first. The blessings are said and then the *shammash* is used to light the other candles. The *shammash* should be slightly higher in the menorah than the other lights so it is clear that it is not one of the regular candles. It should be easy for anyone to see, just by looking at a lit menorah, which night of the holiday is being celebrated.

4. Each person in the household should use the *shammash* to light one candle on the first night, two candles on the second night, adding one each night until the eighth night when eight candles are lit. Each person should light his/her candles separately so that it is clear how many candles each person has lit and what night of Hanukkah is being celebrated. The Hanukkah candles should not be placed where candles are lit throughout the year so that it is clear these are special lights—Hanukkah lights.

Hanukkah Bummer

When your dentist wishes you a happy Hanukkah and then says you have 12 cavities

5. On the first night, the light farthest on the right of the menorah should be lit. On the second night, two lights should be placed in the menorah, beginning with the one farthest to the right, and then lit beginning with the newest one on the left and moving to the right. (See illustration on page 13.)

6. The lights should be in an even row. One candle should not be higher and another lower, and there should be a space between one light and the other so one flame does not merge with another.

7. Two people should not light one menorah at the same time, even on the first night, because it would not be clear from the lights which night of Hanukkah it is.

8. The time to light the Hanukkah candles is as soon as the stars appear, and it should not be postponed. Other than evening prayers, nothing should be done after nightfall until the lights are lit. Everyone in the household should gather together for the lighting. The lights must burn for at least half an hour. If the lights have not been lit right after nightfall, they may be lit as long as some people in the household are awake. If all others in the household are asleep, the lights are lit without reciting the blessings. If someone will not be able to light the candles after nightfall (Erev Shabbat, Friday evening, is such a time), the lights may be lit about one and a quarter hours before the stars appear, but they should then burn at least half an hour after nightfall.

9. On the first night, three blessings are said. (See Blessings on page 6.) On the second night, only the first two. After the blessings are said, the first light is lit. While lighting the others, *Hanerot hallalu* is said. (See *Hanerot hallalu* on page 7.)

10. During the first half hour that the lights burn, the time that fulfills the mitzvah of the lighting, you should not read by the light of the candles or make any other use of the lights. For that reason, the lighting candle, the *shammash*, is left in the menorah. Use may be made of the light from the *shammash*.

11. In the synagogue, Hanukkah lights are lit and the blessings are said between the afternoon (*Mincha*) and evening (*Ma'ariv*) prayers and are then placed near the southern wall of the

temple. People who come to the synagogue for the lighting should still light Hanukkah candles at home. Someone who is in the year of morning for a loved one should not light the Hanukkah candles for the congregation on the first night.

12. After Shabbat, the Hanukkah lights are lit and then *Havdallah* (the prayer marking the end of Shabbat) is said.

13. Someone who is out of town and knows that candles are being lit at home by his/her wife or husband, should light candles wherever he/she is without saying the blessings. It is best, if possible, to hear someone else make the blessings and, while listening, keep in mind the lighting in his/her home. However, if no spouse is lighting candles at home, he/she should light the candles and make the blessings. Someone who is not at home at candle lighting time can also simply wait until he/she arrives home and light the candles then.

14. The lights must be in a doorway or window that can be seen outside the house so that the Hanukkah miracles are publicized. If they are lit near the door, they should be lit on the left side, so that with the mezuzah on the right and the Hanukkah lights on the left, we are surrounded with mitzvot—good deeds.

15. The lights should be higher than three handbreaths (12 inches) above the floor and preferably lower than ten handbreaths (forty inches), but must be lower than twenty cubits (each cubit is about 18 inches). Someone who lives in an apartment may light them near a window, even if the window is higher than ten handbreaths above the ground.

16. All kinds of oil are good for the Hanukkah lights, but olive oil is preferred. If olive oil is not available, another oil that gives a clear and bright flame should be used, or else wax candles because their light is also clear. Two candles must not be stuck together.

17. All kinds of wicks may be used, but cotton is preferred. It is not necessary to use a new wick each night. You may light the original wicks until they are no longer usable, but the lights should burn each night for at least thirty minutes.

Sephardic Customs

Sephardic Jews are those whose ancestors come from Spain, Portugal, the Mediterranean Basin, North Africa, and the Middle East. They sometimes observe Hanukkah differently from Ashkenazic Jews, whose ancestors are from Eastern Europe. For instance:

- In Kurdistan, Iraq, the children prepare an effigy (a crude figure representing a hated person) of Antiochus IV, which is thrown into a bonfire on the last day of Hanukkah.

- In Bukhara, a town in southern Russia, parents make cakes for their children's teachers that have gold and silver coins baked in them.

- In some North African communities, the seventh night of Hanukkah is dedicated to female heroines such as Judith and Hannah. Women gather in the synagogue, take out the Torah, and receive a blessing from the rabbi in the name of the matriarchs.

- To honor female solidarity, girls in Salonika, Greece, who are angry with each other usually resolve their differences during Hanukkah, much as Jews everywhere do on Yom Kippur.

- In Yemen, every child receives a coin each day of Hanukkah. The children usually spend it on a special Hanukkah drink of sugar, water, and red food coloring—"wine"—to be served with a Hanukkah delicacy of peas or lentils.

- Many Sephardic women do not work or do chores during the holiday, especially on the seventh night, to recall the martyrdom of Hannah and the courage of Judith.

The Hanukkah of Adam and Eve: A Talmudic Legend

The man asked the child, "Do you know why the first day of Hanukkah falls on the twenty-fifth of the month of Kislev?"

The child answered, "Because on that day Judah Maccabee drove Antiochus from Jerusalem and restored the Temple. On that day the candles are lit."

"You know that history is an eternal repetition. It may be that there were other important events on that same day. Let us try together to see what they were." After these words the man and the child went back through the course of the centuries until they came at last to the time of Adam and Eve.

The Garden of Eden was flooded with sunlight. The trees were in flower, the birds were singing, the flowers perfumed the air.

But one day Adam listened to the words of Eve and ate of the

Why did the cook run out of the kitchen?

Because the sufganiyot recipe said, "Take one egg and beat it."

Hanukkah Bummer

Frozen latkes

fruit of the forbidden tree. Both of them were then driven from the Garden of Eden and had to earn their bread by the sweat of their brows.

There came a time when Adam noticed that the sun was setting earlier and night fell more quickly. The days grew shorter and the nights grew longer. Was this a new punishment from God?

Frightened, Adam and Eve fasted and prayed. A week went by and the sun still set earlier and earlier. Was it possible that darkness was coming again, little by little over the face of the earth, and that all life would be destroyed?

But then … a miracle! The sun began to remain longer, a little longer each day. The days grew longer and the nights shorter. Adam smiled at his fears.

He and Eve made a feast of rejoicing and lit fires in token of their gratitude. For they knew now that what had been had already taken place and would last forever. The stars sparkled in the heavens. As long as earth endured there would be days, seasons, years, the time of sowing and the time of harvest, heat and cold, day and night.

The day on which Adam lit fires of joy and gratitude fell in the middle of the winter when the sun reaches the point farthest from the center of the earth and begins again on its eternal course.

This is the twenty-fifth day of the month of Kislev.

A Hanukkah Heroine: Judith

There is a story told around the dinner table during Hanukkah about a beautiful woman named Judith who used her wisdom to defeat an enemy of the Jews. The message is clear: Sometimes a woman can win a battle using hidden skills. In honor of Judith's bravery and wise plan, it is customary to eat cheese dishes during Hanukkah time (read on to discover why) and for women to take time off from regular chores and with special blessings in synagogue.

King Holofernes conquered many lands and peoples. One day he decided that he would conquer Jerusalem and the Jewish people and brought his armies up to Jerusalem and surrounded the city. The people saw how strong King Holofernes was and how many soldiers were in his army. They were frightened, and they decided to pray to God and wait five days to see if God would save them.

Living in the city was a pious and beautiful woman named Judith, who heard the news about King Holofernes and his plans to seize Jerusalem. She decided to get to know the king and to use her beauty to seduce him.

Judith traveled to the king's camp and was brought before him. Her beauty immediately struck him. When he asked her the purpose of her visit, she offered to lead him straight into the heart of the city of Jerusalem so that his armies could conquer it quickly. The king was charmed by her apparent wisdom and her offer, and he asked her to dine with him later in the day.

Judith fed King Holofernes a cheese dish, which made him thirsty, and then gave him wine. The king, enjoying himself, drank so much wine that he fell asleep on his bed and Judith had her opportunity to remove this enemy of Israel. She used his own sword to cut off his head. Then she quietly stole away into the night. When word spread of the king's demise, his armies fled in fear, and the city of Jerusalem was at peace once more.

How Billings, Montana, Defended Hanukkah

In 1993, Billings, Montana, suffered from increasing numbers of hate crimes against minorities. Members of an African American church were harassed, the house of a Native American woman was painted with swastikas, a Jewish cemetery was vandalized, and the synagogue received multiple bomb threats. The Ku Klux Klan and the Aryan Nations groups responsible for these hate crimes also distributed thousands of brochures that promoted prejudice and encouraged people to try to get rid of all the minorities in town. After each hate crime, groups of people in Billings came forward to support the victims of the crimes and to help repair damage.

Then, in December, a hate crime against a young Jewish boy brought the whole town together in a mass protest against hate and violence. Right before Hanukkah, Isaac Schnitzer, a six-year-old boy, decorated his bedroom window with a colorful paper menorah. The next day, someone threw a rock through the decorated window. Luckily, no one was hurt, but the Schnitzer family was very upset that someone broke their window just because they were Jewish. The police promised to try to protect the family, but also suggested that they remove the Hanukkah menorah from their window to avoid other attacks. Tammie Schnitzer, a human rights activist and a convert to Judaism, refused to hide her family's Judaism. Instead, she called the local newspaper and said, "Please make this front page news because I want people to understand what it's like to be Jewish."

Immediately, people in the community began to respond. One of Isaac's non-Jewish friends made him a new paper menorah to replace the one that was destroyed. The town held a large meeting of activists, clergy, the press, and the police. At this meeting, one person suggested that Billings should follow the example of Denmark during the Holocaust. Both Jewish and non-Jewish Danes started wearing the yellow star that the Nazis used to identify Jews. The Danish people, led by their king, unified to protect the Jews from discrimination.

Following this suggestion, the newspaper printed a large picture of a menorah and encouraged readers to put the picture in their windows. At first, the schools, churches, and homes that displayed these pictures of Hanukkah menorahs were also vandalized. The Billings Human Rights Network, the police, and the town clergy urged more people to display the newspaper's menorah picture, and, as more and more people put Hanukkah menorahs in their windows, the hate crimes slowly faded. By the end of December, more than 10,000 people in Billings had a menorah in their window.

With this act of support and solidarity, the people of Billings declared that violence and hate crimes would not be accepted or tolerated against Jews or any other minority. They told hate groups, "Not in our town." Although this incident occurred over ten years ago, the message still echoes through the town of Billings and all over the country, as the story is repeated and

The Shammash

by RAHEL MUSLEAH

Rabbi Avi Weiss, of the Hebrew Institute of Riverdale, New York, draws inspiration from the candle that lights the others. "All the candles take light; the *shammash* is the only one that gives," he explains. "There are forces of evil out there, but also great *shammashim*, great human beings who give of themselves. When the *shammash* touches one of the eight candles, the flame becomes greater. We may think that the more we give, the less we have, but difficult circumstances show the opposite. The more we give, the greater the light. The key to the healing process is not to be selfish but to be selfless; not self-protective but protective of others."

spread through books like Janice Cohn's *The Christmas Menorahs: How a Town Fought Hate* (Albert Whitman, 1996). Like the Maccabees, the Jews and non-Jews of the town stood up to those who wished to overpower a minority. They fought for their beliefs, celebrating freedom and the courage of the Maccabees. That Hanukkah, the people of Billings created their own Hanukkah miracle, banding together with small actions to fight against the strength of hate and hate groups.

A Hanukkah Memory
by DAVID A. ADLER

I grew up in a big old house with plenty of room for the eight of us—my parents, my three brothers, my two sisters, and me. Mutti stayed with us, too, for most weekends and Jewish holidays.

"*Mutti*" is German for "Mother," and for us it was fitting that we called her that. She was our grandmother, our mother's mother. But remarkably, virtually everyone who knew her called her Mutti, too. For many years, I didn't know her true first name. It was Alice.

Friends marveled at Mutti's energy. Even in her eighties, she still went regularly to hospitals and nursing homes to visit lonely patients. She called them the "old" people, but most of them were younger than she was.

When Mutti came on Friday for the weekend, for Shabbat, she brought us hand-rolled marzipan, lox wrapped in paper, and often the sort of toys she loved. Among them was a wind-up plastic chicken that laid a plastic egg, and a small bear that walked down a gentle incline.

On Hanukkah, of course, we all played dreidel. Mutti knew the rules of the game, but there was still trouble. My brother Eddie believed in doing things exactly right, and after a few rounds of dreidel he would complain bitterly that Mutti was cheating. I often sat next to her and knew he was right. She did cheat at dreidel—and at most games she played with us. She'd spin a *gimel* and claim it was a *nun*. She'd spin a *hey* and claim it was a *shin*. Mutti didn't need to win. She just wanted her grandchildren to be happy. She cheated so that she would lose and we would win.

To Be a Lamplighter

by MENACHEM MENDEL SCHNEERSON

A Hasid once asked: "Rebbe, what is a Jew's task in this world?"

The rebbe answered: "A Jew is a lamplighter on the streets of the world. In olden days, there was a person in every town who would light the gas streetlamps with a light he carried at the end of a long pole. On the street corners, the lamps were there in readiness, waiting to be lit; a lamplighter had a pole with a flame supplied by the town. He knew that the fire was not his own, and he went around lighting all the lamps on his route."

The Hasid asked: "But what if the lamp is in a desolate wilderness?"

The rebbe answered: "Then, too, one must light it. For let it be noted that there is a wilderness, and let the wilderness feel ashamed before the light."

"But what if the lamp is in the midst of the sea?"

"Then one must take off one's clothes, jump into the water, and light it there!"

"And that is the Jew's mission?"

The rebbe thought for a long moment and then said: "Yes, that is a Jew's calling."

The Hasid continued: "Rebbe, I see no lamps!"

The rebbe answered: "That is because you are not yet a lamplighter."

The Hasid asked: "How does one become a lamplighter?"

The rebbe replied: "One must begin with oneself, cleansing oneself, becoming more refined, then one sees the other as a source of light, waiting to be ignited. When, Heaven forbid, one is crude, then one sees crudeness; but when one is noble, one sees nobility."

When we lead a righteous life, we can see the righteousness of others and the light in their soul. The rebbe here is explaining that Jews have the responsibility to look past their own problems and selfishness and go around spreading the light of Torah and mitzvot to others. The Bible teaches that "the com-

The Olympics and the Maccabiah

Did you know that the word "Maccabiah" comes from the word "Maccabees"? The Maccabiah Games are the Jewish version of the Olympics, and they take place around the world. Jewish athletes participate in nearly every area of sports competition. The first world Jewish Olympics were held in 1932 and included 500 participants from 23 countries. Three years later, in 1935, 1,700 athletes joined together in the Maccabiah Games after being excluded from the Olympics that were held in Nazi Germany in 1936.

Though the modern Olympics have much in common with the Maccabiah Games, the ancient Olympics were actually considered pagan festivals. The Olympics originated in Olympia, Greece, where a competition to honor the Greek god Zeus included sports like discus throwing and chariot racing. The winners didn't receive a gold medal; they were honored with an olive wreath. The ancient society valued the strength and beauty of the body, almost to the point of worshiping the human form. Athletes competed to achieve glory and immortality.

Modern times bring a different set of values to the Olympics and to the Maccabiah Games. Both encourage teamwork and healthy competition—being a good sport is very important. Athletes treat each other with respect and pride. Being part of a delegation is a great honor and a position reached only after intense national competitions. Many athletes become national heroes, admired for their courage and determination. Perhaps this is the same kind of admiration the ancient Maccabees received from the Jews when the Temple of Jerusalem was rededicated.

mandment (mitzvah) is a lamp, the teaching is a light" (Prov. 6:23) and that "the life breath of man is the lamp of the Lord." A lamplighter is one who uses the light of teaching to kindle people's souls, no matter where those people are and how difficult it might be to reach them. A Jew must be someone who will sacrifice some personal comfort to go out in search of those who need to be ignited. In this way, a Jew practices *tikkun olam*, improving the world, and shares the joy and light of the Torah and mitzvot.

Hanukkah in 1944, A True Story

by RUTH MINSKY SENDER

Hanukkah, 1944. I was in a German concentration camp. We were 50 girls in a crowded room lined with triple-decker wooden bunks. A table and a few benches stood in the center. Each night, we were left in this room after a hard day in a German factory. We were hungry and bruised and we would crawl into our dark cubicles to cry, and to dream of freedom and food.

One night, weak and hopeless, we were all laying on our sacks of straw. A head poked out from the narrow opening of the bunk on the other end of the room. Sara, one of the older girls, looked toward the little window and the barbed wire beyond. She sighed and said softly, *"Kinder, es is Chanuke"* (Children, it's Hanukkah). For a few moments there was silence. Then, one by one, more heads slipped out from the cubicles. Memories of Hanukkah with mothers, fathers, sisters, and brothers started coming back. *"Oy vey,"* said Rose, "if I had my mama's latkes right now," and with tears in her voice, she added "... if I had my mama...."

From the top bunk we heard the whisper of a Hanukkah song: *"O, ir kleine likhtelekh"* (O, you tiny little candle lights). Somehow strengthened by an inner flame, we all joined in, singing together with tears in our eyes: *"Ir dertseylt fun mutikayt, wunder fun amol"* (You tell of bravery and wonders long ago. Jews, there were battles you waged. Jews, there were victories. All so hard to believe.) At that moment the German guard outside the room began to bang on the door with her rifle. "Stop that or I will come in," she shouted. We stopped, but I smiled and whispered to my friend, "We have just won a victory. We are still alive, we will survive!"

Today, when I think back to that Hanukkah night, I see another great miracle before me. I see the children who, according to Hitler's master plan, should never have been born.

But here we are: myself, a survivor, who teaches the children to be proud of their Jewishness, and the new generation who will learn, I hope, to draw strength and courage from the Maccabees of long ago and the Maccabees of our own time.

How Did the Story of Hanukkah End?

You probably know how the story of Hanukkah began. Cruel King Antiochus IV was king of the Syrian empire. He ruled over the Jews and forbade them to practice their religion. King Antiochus sacrificed unkosher animals in the Holy Temple and kept idols there. Whenever he found a Jew keeping a Jewish commandment he had him killed!

Judah Maccabee and his four brothers stood up to King Antiochus. They collected a small army. On the twenty-fifth of Kislev, Judah and his army entered the Holy Temple and removed King Antiochus' idols and unkosher animals. The Macabees restored the Temple as a place where God could be properly served again.

But the story of Hanukkah doesn't end here.

The war between the Syrians and the Jews continued for 23 more years. When King Antiochus died, his son took over the kingdom, and he was even crueler to the Jews. They still were not allowed to practice their religion.

Over the years, the Maccabee brothers were all killed in battle except for one, Simeon. He led the Jewish army and served in the Temple as the high priest, and the Jews finally won the war. At last, they were able to practice their religion as they wanted.

Miracles for a Broken Planet

by CHAIM POTOK

Hanukkah is the Festival of Lights. It commemorates an ancient Jewish rebellion against oppression, during which the Temple in Jerusalem was miraculously recaptured from pagan hellenizers and rededicated to the worship of God. The candles of Hanukkah celebrate that rededication. They also help brighten the long winter nights.

But I remember a Hanukkah when darkness almost overpowered the light. It was the first week of November 1938. The final years of the Depression lay like a polluting mist across the streets of New York. On afternoons when it did not rain I would play on the sidewalk in front of the plate-glass window of the candy store near our apartment house. The bubble of darkness on the other side of the world bumped only vaguely against my consciousness.

I was very young then, interested more in Flash Gordon and Buck Rogers than Adolf Hitler.

One afternoon I was near the candy store, in the cardboard box that was my rocket ship, when an elderly couple walked slowly by; I caught some of their frightening words. Before supper that evening I saw my mother standing over the kitchen sink, her head bowed, and heard her whispering agitatedly to herself. Later, my father came home from work, drenched in weariness; he turned on the radio and became wearier still.

That night I lay awake in my bed and saw the pieces of the day come together and form a portrait of terror. "A Jewish boy had shot a German official in Paris," the old people had said. "We will pay dearly for it, very dearly." "The boy had been sent by his parents to live with his uncle in Paris," my father had murmured. "Then the boy's parents were deported to Poland by the Nazis in Germany."

"The boy went out of his mind," my mother had said in a voice full of fear. "He did not know what he was doing."

I lay very still in my bed, thinking of the boy who had shot the German and wondering what the Germans would do to the Jews. Two days later the German official died, then came Krystal Nacht, the pogroms called the Night of the Broken Glass, November 9, 1938.

In the weeks that followed, I dreamed about the synagogues that were burning all over Germany, about the Jews who were being sent to concentration camps, about the looted stores and smashed shop windows. One day I stood in front of our apartment house and imagined our street littered with glass, shattered glass everywhere, the plate-glass window of the candy store shattered across the sidewalk, the store itself burned and gutted. I imagined the entire block, the neighborhood, the city heaped with broken glass and thick with the stench of fire. The days of that November and December began to go dark, until it seemed all the world would soon be shades of darkness: dark sun and dark moon, dark sky and dark earth, dark night and dark day. I was a child then, but I still remember that darkness as a malevolence I could touch and smell, an evil growth draining my world of its light.

My world seemed thick with that darkness when Hanukkah came that year on the twenty-fifth of December. I remember my father chanting the blessings over the first candle on the first night of the festival. He was short and balding, and he chanted in a thin, intense voice. I stood between him and my mother, gazing at the flame of the first night's candle. The flame seemed pitiful against the malignant darkness outside our window. I went to bed and was cold with dread over the horror of the world.

The next night, two candles were lighted. Again my father chanted the blessings before the lighting and the prayer that follows when the candles are burning: "We kindle these lights on account of the miracles, the deliverances, and the wonders which You did for our ancestors. . . . During all eight days of Hanukkah these lights are sacred. . . . We are only to look at them, in order that we may give thanks unto Your Name, for Your miracles, Your deliverances, and Your wonders."

I wanted a miracle. But there were no miracles during that Hanukkah. Where was God? I kept dreaming of burning synagogues.

On the eighth and final night of the festival I stood with my parents in front of the burning candles. The darkness mocked their light. I could see my parents glancing at me. My mother sighed. Then my father murmured my name.

"You want another miracle?" he asked wearily.

I did not respond.

"Yes," he said. "You want another miracle." He was silent a moment. Then he said, in a gentle, urgent voice, "I also want another miracle. But if it does not come, we will make a human miracle. We will give the world the special gifts of our Jewishness. We will not let the world burn out our souls."

The candles glowed feebly against the dark window.

"Sometime I think man is a greater miracle-maker than God," my father said tiredly, looking at the candles. "God does not have to live day after day on this broken planet. Perhaps you will learn to make your own miracles. I will try to teach you how to make human miracles."

I lay awake a long time that night and did not believe my father could ever teach me that. But now, decades later, I think he taught me well. And I am trying hard to teach it to my own children.

PART
Two

The Little Hanukkah Lamp

by I. L. PERETZ

translated and adapted by
ESTHER HAUTZIG

This classic story will delight older readers.

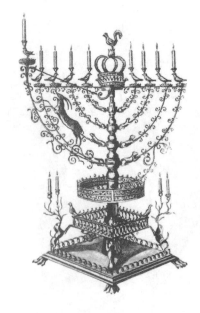

Many years ago a God-fearing Jew named Shloime-Zalmen was saved by his little Hanukkah lamp. You think perhaps that the lamp was made of gold or silver? On the contrary; this old, broken relic was made of brass. Decorated with birds on trees and a laughing lion, this ancient keepsake must have been handed down from generation to generation. It was twisted and shapeless, with one candleholder missing, but Shloime-Zalmen and his family lit Hanukkah candles in it for years.

Shloime-Zalmen had a little business of his own in Warsaw. One day he met a soldier selling iron bars on the street and became a very rich man, practically a millionaire! Shloime-Zalmen bought the iron bars very cheaply. When he brought the iron bars home, he polished them with a metal file. Imagine what he found beneath the iron. Gold! Maybe stolen from a bank?

And when this Jew became rich, everything turned topsy-turvy in his household. He changed his name. Shloime-Zalmen became Mr. Solomon. He changed his appearance. Shloime-Zalmen—or rather Mr. Solomon—threw away all his old-fashioned clothes and became a dandy. His wife threw away her wig, the *sheitel* she had worn for years, bought new dresses, and tried to look like a French model.

Their two sons were taken out of religious school, the *heder*, and enrolled in a gymnasium, a private school for the nonobservant.

The Solomons transformed their household. Their special bookcase for holy books? Who needed holy books? Mr. Solomon and his wife gave them to the house of study, to the *beit midrash*. The bookcase, an old piece of furniture, was chopped up for kindling! Mrs. Solomon replaced the bookcase with a full-length mirror. Suddenly she liked to look at her reflection, to admire herself.

The Solomons called in the junk dealer and sold all their furniture for practically nothing. Next they bought antiques—Louis XIV furnishings! Small, charming, upholstered, on twisted legs trimmed with gilt. Light, movable, fragile—a pleasure to behold. No one dared to sit down!

Some old silver still remained—small boxes, spice containers. Valuable antiques, yet they sold them for pennies. Some they gave

30

away as wedding gifts to relatives. The little Hanukkah lamp was stashed away. Who cared about an old, broken relic? They bought glass, crystal, flowerpots, and vases, all to keep up with the customs of the modern world.

Years went by.

Since the world turns round and round, things turned upside down for Mr. Solomon—buttered side down. His business failed. His creditors refused to wait any longer for their money. Another loan was out of the question. He had no money to send to his sons, who by that time studied abroad.

Things went from bad to worse. Mr. Solomon and his wife searched their house. "Isn't there anything to pawn?" he asked. The Louis XIV furniture, so fine, so fragile, was in ruins. The glass and crystal were chipped and broken. The few remaining flowerpots were cracked, barely held together with plaster. "We haven't anything to pawn," said his wife.

The couple lived on in dire poverty. And when they lived in poverty, they remembered their Jewishness. The wife borrowed a copy of the Pentateuch from a neighbor and read it. Mr. Solomon, once again called Shloime-Zalmen, put on his prayer shawl and tefillin and prayed.

Hanukkah Bummer

When your uncle gives you Hanukkah gelt and it's play money

When Hanukkah came around, Shloime-Zalmen and his wife felt a great desire to celebrate it, make the benediction, light the candles. Somehow they got the little candles. They tried to find in their kitchen a slab of wood on which to place the candles. There was none, not even a bit of kindling.

"Once, long, long ago, we had an old Hanukkah lamp which I threw on top of our stove," Shloime-Zalmen remembered.

"Take it down," his wife begged Sholime-Zalmen.

Risking life and limb, they put a bench on top of the rickety Louis XIV table. They shoved the table close to the stove. The table trembled and squeaked. One could almost hear Louis XIV groan! Shloime-Zalmen climbed on top of the bench that stood on top of the table, which his wife held for dear life. They got down the little Hanukkah lamp.

The lamp was covered with grime and soot. The old couple

could barely get it clean. At last they could light the candles and say the benediction.

On the first day of Hanukkah, the second day, the third, Shloime-Zalmen lit the candles and said the prayers. Afterward he sat at one end of the table, his wife at the other, and they contemplated their sad fate. There was no food, there was no wine. Some nights they thought they would surely die of hunger.

One evening, as they sat at the empty table, their doorbell rang. Shloime-Zalmen and his wife jumped up and opened the door. A young man they knew, a dealer in all manner of goods, came in laughing until tears rolled down his cheeks. "What is the matter?" asked Shloime-Zalmen.

The young man could hardly stop. "A crazy man came to Warsaw from England. Clean-shaven! Perhaps a woman in disguise? He is buying all sorts of old things, even broken relics. He is waiting in the lobby."

The old couple looked at each other.

"Should he come in? Perhaps something will turn up. After all, this is an old household."

Shloime-Zalmen and his wife exchanged looks again. What old things did they own that anyone would want? The Englishman, impatient to get on with his business, walked in. After all, their door was open. He took off his fur coat. He noticed the little Hanukkah lamp and fell upon it like a hungry man falls upon a hot pancake. He held it with trembling hands. His eyes sparkled.

"How much? How much?" asked the Englishman in broken German.

"Didn't I tell you he is crazy?" whispered the young man.

To make a long story short, Shloime-Zalmen and his wife sold the little Hanukkah lamp. They depended entirely on the Englishman's sense of fairness and accepted whatever he offered.

The Englishman and the young man went away. Shloime-Zalmen and his wife remained at home, dumbfounded.

"Crazy!" said Shloime-Zalmen.

"Perhaps it was Elijah the Prophet who paid us a visit because we lit the Hanukkah candles," said his wife with some hesitation.

Shloime-Zalmen and his wife had enough money for supper that night, for breakfast the next morning, and for going to market as well.

Greetings from Echo Canyon

The money they got for the Hanukkah lamp proved lucky. The wheel of fortune turned again for Shloime-Zalmen and his wife—this time buttered side up. Letters with good news came from their sons abroad. They had done well in the world. The son in London had become an engineer. He had gotten married. He wanted his parents to visit so they could meet their daughter-in-law.

Shloime-Zalmen and his wife went to England. After spending happy days with their son and daughter-in-law in their home, they went to see the sights of London—houses, factories, theaters, concert halls, exhibits. Their daughter-in-law took them to an art museum. Imagine their astonishment when they came face-to-face with their old Hanukkah lamp displayed in a glass case! They recognized the old laughing lion, the trees with the birds, the twisted leg, the half-broken candleholder.

Maybe the Englishman wasn't crazy? thought Mr. Solomon in England.

Maybe it wasn't Elijah the Prophet, thought his wife.

To talk loudly, to ask questions, did not seem proper in the museum, and certainly not in front of their young daughter-in-law. So they just thought. Maybe you, dear reader, will want to think about it, too?

Malke's Secret Recipe

by DAVID A. ADLER

Illustrated by AVI KATZ

In Chelm, as in other towns, each family had its own latke recipe. In some families the recipe had been handed down from mother to daughter for many generations. Some people added just salt and pepper to the potatoes. Others added eggs and onions. There were even people who added paprika, parsley, and bread crumbs.

Most people were happy to share their latke recipes. But not Malke, the tailor's wife. "I may be a poor woman," Malke said, "but I make the best latkes in Chelm, and I'm the only one who has the recipe."

When Malke was a young bride, she would let people taste her latkes. She wanted everyone to know how good they were. But Malke soon became afraid that someone eating them might be able to taste each ingredient and learn her recipe. Since then, she only let her husband and children eat her famous latkes.

As the years passed, Malke's latkes tasted even better in people's memories than they had on their forks. Berel, the shoemaker, always closed his eyes and smiled when he remembered Malke's latkes. "They were so very soft," he would tell his wife, Yentel, "and so very light. Eating Malke's latkes was like eating a cloud."

Then one Hanukkah night, Berel, Yentel, and their children were eating latkes. These were not soft and light, but thick, heavy ones. Berel took one bite and banged on the table. "Enough!" he shouted. "I'm tired of the same latkes every Hanukkah. Tomorrow I'm getting Malke's recipe."

The next morning Berel told Yentel, "I'm not opening the shop today. If someone comes with his shoes, tell him to come back tomorrow. But don't tell him where I've gone."

Berel hid behind a tree near Malke's house. He waited there all day, but Malke didn't make latkes. That night, Berel watched as Malke and her family lit their Hanukkah candles. He heard them sing "Maoz Tzur," and he watched them play dreidel.

Then Berel saw Malke take out some potatoes, a grater, and a large pan.

Hanukkah Bummer

"Yuch!"

Left-over latkes and watery applesauce

"This is it!" Berel said to himself. "Tonight I will eat latkes as soft and light as a cloud."

Berel crawled close to the window. He watched and wrote down everything Malke did. When the latkes were done, Berel ran home to his wife Yentel.

"I've got it!" he said. "I've got Malke's recipe."

Berel looked at his paper. "First take five potatoes and two eggs," he read.

"Some secret recipe," Yentel said as she watched Berel peel the potatoes. "We always use potatoes and eggs."

Berel grated the potatoes into a bowl. He added the eggs. "We do that, too," Yentel said.

"Now," Berel read, "chop six scallions very fine."

"Scallions!" Yentel said. "Who ever heard of using scallions in latkes? Everyone uses an onion. An onion is better."

"So I'll use an onion," Berel said. He chopped it and mixed it in with the potatoes.

"Next," Berel said, "Malke mixed in flour."

"Don't use flour. Use bread crumbs," Yentel said.

So Berel used breadcrumbs. Then he added some salt. He looked down at his paper and was about to add pepper when

Why did Eli celebrate Hanukkah only on Shabbat and Sunday?

He was told to light candles only on the wick ends.

Yentel shook her head and said, "Pepper makes me sneeze."

So Berel didn't add the pepper.

"Now I need a lemon," Berel said. "Malke squeezed in a few drops of lemon juice."

Yentel shook her head. "No. Lemon juice belongs in tea."

"And Malke added parsley," Berel continued. "She made her latkes very thin and fried them in vegetable oil."

"Parsley! Vegetable oil! That's not a secret recipe. That's secret nonsense," Yentel said. "Parsley belongs in a salad with carrots. In this house we fry in chicken fat. And thick latkes taste better than thin ones."

Berel and Yentel made their latkes with potatoes, eggs, salt, and breadcrumbs, just like they always did. They made their latkes very thick and fried them in chicken fat.

When the latkes were done, Berel and Yentel and their children sat down to eat them. They ate slowly. They wanted to know if Malke's latkes really did taste better than anyone else's.

"These latkes don't taste soft and light," one of the children said.

"And they don't taste like clouds," another added.

"Some secret recipe," Berel told Yentel after all the latkes were eaten. "They taste just like ours."

"Well," Yentel said, "this just proves that no matter how you make them, latkes always taste the same."

K'tonton Takes a Ride on a Runaway Dreidel

by SADIE ROSE WEILERSTEIN

Illustrated by MARILYN HIRSH

Here's a classic story that will delight younger readers.

It was Hanukkah, the Feast of Lights. The first little Hanukkah light was shining in the window. Aunt Gittel and Uncle Israel had come to visit. So had the little old *bubbe*. You remember her, don't you? The little old woman who sat next to K'tonton's mother in synagogue and told her what to do if she wanted to have a child! From the kitchen came the pleasant sizzle, sizzle of frying latkes. Everyone was laughing and singing and chattering—everyone but K'tonton. K'tonton sat in a corner by himself as sober as a weekday. There wasn't a smile on his face, not the tiniest bit of a smile. And all because of his great ambition. He had told the lions on the Hanukkah menorah all about that ambition the day before.

"See my *tzedakah* box—the blue one with the white star. It's where I put my charity. I'm going to fill it to the very top. Clinkety, clink, away the pennies will go to Israel! They're to buy land, you know—for the Jewish farmers there, the *halutzim*. They ought to get a good piece of land with a whole box full of money."

But, of course, if K'tonton wanted to fill his box, he had to have Hanukkah gelt, coins given to children for Hanukkah. But no one in the room had offered him any, not Father, not Mother, not Bubbe, not Uncle Israel or Aunt Gittel.

"Maybe they're hungry and that makes them forget," thought K'tonton. "Perhaps they'll remember after they've had their latkes." But no! Mother brought the latkes in— a great plateful of potato pancakes for the grownups, a tiny plateful for K'tonton. Every latke was eaten and still no one said a word about Hanukkah gelt.

"Perhaps I should remind them," thought K'tonton. "I'll go right up and I'll say, 'Don't you know it's Hanukkah? Don't you know you're supposed to give Hanukkah gelt on Hanukkah?'"

But no. It wouldn't be polite to ask for Hanukkah gelt.

"Come here, my little sober one," called Uncle Israel, picking K'tonton up in his hand. "Where's your Hanukkah smile? Get the dreidel, Gittel! We've got to wake our K'tonton up."

K'tonton Arrives

The following passage is an excerpt from Sadie Rose Weilerstein's classic story, "K'tonton Arrives." Read on to understand why our friend is so tiny!

Once upon a time there lived a husband a wife. They had everything in the world to make them happy, or almost everything ... Only one thing was missing and that was a child.

"Ah," the woman would sigh, "if only I could have a child! I shouldn't mind if he were no bigger than a thumb."

One day—it was Sukkot, the Feast of Tabernacles—she was praying in the synagogue, when she happened to look down. There at her side stood a little old woman. Such a queer, wrinkled old woman with deep, kind eyes peering up at her from under a shawl!

"Why do you look so sad," asked the old woman, "and why do you pray so earnestly?"

"I am sad," answered the wife, "because I have no child. Ah, that I might have a child! I shouldn't mind if he were no bigger than a thumb."

"In that case," said the little old woman, "I shall tell you what to do. Has your husband an *etrog*?"

"Indeed he has," said the wife.

"Then," said the old woman, "on the last day of Sukkot you must take the etrog and bite off the end, and you shall have your wish."

The wife thanked the little old woman kindly. When the last day of Sukkot came, she bit off the end of the *etrog* just as she had been told. Sure enough, before the year had passed a little baby was born to her. It was a dear little boy baby, with black eyes and black hair, dimples in his knees, and thumbs just right for sucking. There was only one strange thing about him. He was exactly the size of a thumb, not one bit smaller or larger.

The wife laughed when she saw him. I don't know whether she laughed because she was so glad or because it seemed so funny to have a baby as big as a thumb. Whichever it was, the husband said, "We shall call him Isaac, because Isaac means laughter." Then, because they were so thankful to God for sending him, they gave the baby a second name, Samuel. But, of course, you couldn't call such a wee little baby, a baby no bigger than a thumb, Isaac Samuel all the time. So for every day they called him K'tonton, which means very, very little; and that's exactly what he was.

Out came the dreidel, the whirling Hanukkah top with Hebrew letters on the sides. Uncle Israel seated K'tonton on it. Whirl! Twirl! And K'tonton and the Ha-nukkah dreidel were spinning about on the table. Round and round, round and round whirled the dreidel. Faster and faster, faster and faster, faster and faster! Then slower and slower and slower! It swayed. It stopped. K'tonton peered over the side.

"*Gimel!*" he called. His cheeks were rosy with excitement. He had forgotten his disappointment, or almost forgotten it.

"Your turn, Aunt Gittel!" he called.

Whirl, twirl! The dreidel was off again. Straight across the table it went with K'tonton on it.

"Watch out!" cried Father. "It's going over the side."

And over the side it went. Down from the table, across the floor, out through the doorway! Spin, bump! Spin, bump! Down the stairs and out into the street! Down the stairs and out into the street after the runaway dreidel went Father! And after Father, Mother, and after Mother, Uncle Israel and Bubbe and Aunt Gittel.

"Stop the dreidel! Stop it! Stop it!" called Father to a fat policeman at the corner.

"Stop it! Please stop it!" called Mother, who was almost in tears.

"Stop it! Stop the dreidel!" cried Bubbe and Aunt Gittel and Uncle Israel all together.

But the policeman didn't know what a dreidel was.

On and on sped the Hanukkah top with K'tonton holding fast. He laughed aloud. He was enjoying the ride. Now they were at the corner. Now they had turned the corner and were spinning on— down a dark alley, around another corner, on and on and on. And still the dreidel spun. Would it ever stop? K'tonton was not laughing now. Perhaps this was a punishment. Hadn't he sulked about the Hanukkah gelt? Hadn't he spoiled the joy of the holiday with his frown? He must accept whatever befell him.

"*Gam zu l'tovah,*" said K'tonton. "This, too, is for the best!"

As he spoke the dreidel swerved. It turned into a gutter. It swayed drunkenly. It stopped. K'tonton sprang to his feet and looked about. Something was gleaming in the darkness. It wasn't—it couldn't be—but it was! A big, round, shining quarter!

Up came Father panting and out of breath. He stooped over

Hanukkah Bummer

Your aunt gives you Hanukkah gelt and your parents make you give it back

the gutter to pick up his frightened K'tonton. But K'ton-ton wasn't frightened. He was laughing and hugging the shining quarter to his breast.

"Hanukkah gelt, Father!" cried K'tonton, "For my *tzedakah box*."

"Hanukkah gelt?" said Father. "I forgot all about Hanukkah gelt!"

Up came Mother with her handkerchief ready to wipe away K'tonton's tears. But there were no tears to wipe away.

"Hanukkah gelt?" said Mother. "I forgot all about Hanukkah gelt!"

Up came Uncle Israel and Aunt Gittel and the little old *bubbe*. "Hanukkah gelt, Uncle Israel! See my Hanukkah gelt, Bubbe, Aunt Gittel!" And K'tonton held his precious quarter high.

"Hanukkah gelt!" cried Bubbe and Aunt Gittel and Uncle Israel together. "To think we forgot all about Hanukkah gelt!"

Then Father picked up his little son and carried him home, dreidel, Hanukkah gelt, and all, down the street, up the stairs into the house, straight to the big blue and white *tzedakah* box. High up to the top of the box K'tonton was lifted. And then … and …

Then …

Father emptied his pockets. He emptied every penny, nickel, quarter, and dime that was in them. And Uncle Israel emptied his pockets. And Mother and Aunt Gittel emptied their pocketbooks. And the little old bubbe took out her handkerchief and untied the knot in the corner and shook out eight shining new pennies, one for each night of the holiday. The Hanukkah gelt was piled up at the side of the blue box so high it covered the star. Father handed up the coins and K'tonton rolled up his sleeves and pushed each one down the slot of the *tzedakah* box.

"Hurray!" cried K'tonton as the last Hanukkah coin went clinkety, clink, clink into the box. "Hurray for Hanukkah gelt! Hurray for *Eretz Yisrael*! Hurray for the runaway dreidel!"

Hanukkah Bummer

Leaky sufganiyot

Hanukkah Lights

by JOHANNA HURWITZ

There were so many reasons the Hirsch family looked forward to celebrating Hanukkah. Mr. Hirsch liked to retell the historic tale of the brave Maccabees and the scant oil supply, which miraculously burned for eight days. Mrs. Hirsch enjoyed making potato pancakes and homemade doughnuts. Because both foods were cooked in oil, they had become associated with the Hanukkah holiday. And even though she didn't usually prepare fried foods, she made this exception because Hanukkah came only once a year.

"But it lasts for eight days!" shouted Nathan, who was seven years old. "It's better than a birthday!" Nathan looked forward to receiving presents, which was another tradition that had come to be associated with Hanukkah.

"Don't forget the candles," Rebecca said. She was nine and loved presents and potato pancakes with applesauce. But she loved the candles best of all.

Every year, just before the holiday, the Hirsch family bought a new box of Hanukkah candles. There were 44 candles in the box, exactly enough for all eight nights. The first night, the family lit the *shammash* candle and with it lit the first candle in the special Hanukkah menorah. On the second night, they lit two candles and the *shammash*. Each night, one more candle was added to the menorah until the last evening, with eight candles plus the *shammash* burning together to make the most wonderful glow in the window.

Even though the eighth night was the final night of the holiday and she would then have to wait a whole year until Hanukkah returned, Rebecca decided that the eighth night was her favorite.

Hanukkah candles were a special size. They were larger than birthday candles but much smaller than the candles they used on Friday evenings at the start of Shabbat. Rebecca liked to take all 44 candles out of the box and arrange them by color. Until a new box was opened, she never knew what the distribution of colors might be. How many would be red? Or blue? How many yellow candles would there be this year? The children took turns putting the candles in the menorah. When it was Nathan's turn, he just pulled any colors out of the box. But Rebecca liked to plan it so that every evening there would be a mix of colors. She liked to use a yellow candle for the *shammash* and then, if possible, have each other candle be a different color—pink, red, blue, green, white—before starting over again.

This year it was Rebecca's turn to place the candles in the menorah on the final night of Hanukkah. Because it fell on a Sunday, she didn't have to wait until she came home from school to put the candles in place. She did it right after breakfast, and as she did, she anticipated how beautiful they would look when they were all burning together that evening.

After lunch, Rebecca's friend Eva came over to play. She brought her roller skates, and the two girls, and Nathan, too, bundled up and went skating in the park, which was only a couple of blocks from their home.

"Guess what we're going to do this evening," Eva said to Rebecca.

"Have a Hanukkah party?" Rebecca guessed. She thought that perhaps her friend's family had invited their relatives to come and celebrate the conclusion of the holiday with them.

"You're almost right," Eva said. "We're making a little party at the hospital where my grandmother is. We're even going to bring our menorah and light candles in her room."

"That's so nice," said Rebecca. "It will make her feel good."

"My mother said it will be better than medicine," said Eva,

laughing. "I hope so—then she can come home again!" Eva's grandmother lived with Eva, and Rebecca knew that she had been in the hospital for almost two weeks.

At four o'clock, the three kids left the park and Eva went home. Rebecca decided to practice her piano lesson while she waited for sunset. As she played the exercises her teacher had assigned her, she could smell the potato pancakes frying in the kitchen. Her mother didn't make pancakes every night of the holiday, but she always cooked them on the first and last nights. Rebecca inhaled deeply, enjoying the delicious aroma that filled the air. She smiled to herself as she played the notes.

Over the sound of the piano, Rebecca heard another sound. It was their doorbell. She jumped up and went to see who was there. It was Eva.

"Oh, the silliest thing happened at my house," Eva told her. "Our dog, Susie, ate all the Hanukkah candles!"

"She did?" asked Rebecca in amazement. "Will she get sick?" "Probably not. She's always eating things that she shouldn't," Eva answered. "But the problem is, we don't have any more candles. And there's no place open where we can buy some now. Do you have some extra ones that we can use?"

Mrs. Hirsch had come from the kitchen to see who was at the door, and she heard the end of Eva's request.

"Oh, that's too bad," she said. "We have just the right amount for tonight, but no others, I'm afraid. Why doesn't your family come over here and we can light the candles together."

"It will be like a party," Rebecca added eagerly.

"We can't do that," said Eva. And then Rebecca remembered that Eva and her parents had other plans.

"We're going to visit my grandmother at the hospital," Eva continued. "We wanted to bring candles and a menorah to light in her room."

Mrs. Hirsh nodded. "What a shame."

"Couldn't we cut our candles in half?" suggested Rebecca.

"They'd be a lot smaller and they won't burn for very long, but at least we'd have enough, and we can fill both menorahs that way."

"What a clever idea!" Mrs. Hirsch said. "Come. I'll do it at once."

Rebecca and Eva watched as Mrs. Hirsch removed the colorful candles from the menorah and carefully sliced each one in half. She had to use a knife to cut through the wax and then scissors to cut each wick in half. Eva gathered up her share of the small pieces of candle.

"Thanks very, very much," she said. "I know my grandmother is going to be happy when she sees the menorah."

Mrs. Hirsch ran into the kitchen and wrapped up a few latkes for Eva to take along, too. "It isn't Hanukkah without these," she said. "Give your grandmother our love and tell her we hope she's home very soon."

Rebecca put the little stubs of candles into the menorah. She knew that when they were lit they would burn out very quickly. Still, even though she had looked forward to seeing them glowing in the dark, she was pleased that Eva's grandmother would have a chance to share the candles, too.

A little later, Rebecca lit the tiny *shammash* and chanted the blessing over the other little Hanukkah candles. The family sang all their favorite holiday songs as the little lights flickered and burned. Then they sat down at the table and ate their meal. There was pot roast and carrots and latkes with applesauce.

Afterward, when the food was cleared away, Mrs. Hirsch brought out the dreidel, the Hanukkah top. They sat around the table taking turns spinning it. Depending on which side of the dreidel landed on top, the players could win or lose. Sometimes they played with nuts, while other times they played with pennies. But because this was the last night of the holiday, Mr. Hirsch produced a roll of dimes from his pocket and gave them out as prizes. By the end of the game, Rebecca had won 17 dimes and Nathan had won 9.

Rebecca looked over at the window. The menorah was still burning brightly. How could that be? Usually the candles burned all the way down within a half an hour. Tonight, though they were half the size they usually were, they had been burning for over two hours. It was just like a miracle.

Hanukkah Bummer

A latke sandwich

Every year at Hanukkah time, Tante Golda would reach into her wooden barrel and pick out eight of the biggest potatoes she could find. Then she would peel them and grate them and fry them into the most delicious potato latkes in all of Russia.

Her friends and neighbors would crowd into Tante Golda's little kitchen to taste her famous latkes. Tante Golda was never happier than when she stood in front of her black iron stove and cooked batch after batch of golden, crispy latkes and served them to her guests.

"Tante Golda," her guests would say, "these are the most delicious latkes in all of Russia, but you should have saved the potatoes for yourself. There's still a long, cold winter ahead."

"Don't worry about me," Tante Golda would say. "God will provide."

And God did provide. Somehow, Tante Golda's friends and neighbors always managed to drop off a few potatoes now and then, so there was always enough to last her through the winter.

But one year, because of a severe drought, very few potatoes were harvested. When Hanukkah time came around and Tante Golda reached into her wooden barrel, she found only one tiny potato.

"This is terrible!" Tante Golda exclaimed. "Tonight's the first night of Hanukkah—the night I invite all my friends and neighbors over for potato latkes—and I'm down to my last potato!"

She ran next door to her neighbor Risel to see if she had any extra potatoes.

"I'm sorry, Tante Golda. I don't even have one," Risel said.

So Tante Golda ran down the road to her friend Gittel. But Gittel didn't have any either.

Finally, Tante Golda ran across town to her cousin Hodel, but even Hodel's barrel was empty.

Tante Golda held up her one tiny potato.

"I ask you, Hodel, how can I make a Hanukkah party with one tiny potato?"

"You can't," Hodel said, "unless you're a magician."

"A magician I'm not," Tante Golda sighed.

"Then it will have to be a Hanukkah party without potato latkes," Hodel said.

Hodel's husband Moishe looked up from his reading.

The Miracle of the Potato Latkes

MALKA PENN

Illustrated by GIORA CARMI

"A Hanukkah party without Tante Golda's potato latkes! No one would feel like celebrating."

"I guess you're right," Tante Golda reluctantly agreed. "There can't be a Hanukkah party without potato latkes."

Sadly, Tante Golda trudged home. For the first time that she could remember there would be no Hanukkah party, no guests filling her house, no golden, crispy latkes.

But as she lit the first Hanukkah candle, and she remembered the ancient miracle of the oil that lasted for eight days, her face brightened.

"God has always provided," she reassured herself. "Maybe God will provide a miracle now."

Just then, there was a knock on the door. An old beggar was standing there, tired and hungry.

"Is this the miracle?" she asked herself. "A beggar wanting food when I hardly have enough for myself?" But of course, she took pity on the poor beggar.

"I was just about to make a potato latke—or two," she told him. "Won't you come in and join me?"

Naturally, the beggar accepted. He entered Tante Golda's small kitchen and bowed.

"Blessings on you, dear lady. I thought tonight I would surely go hungry. But as I always say, 'God will provide.'"

"Oh, do you say that, too?" Tante Golda asked him. "Well, then, it must be true. Tonight He's provided me with a guest!"

Tante Golda began peeling and grating her one small potato. She added quite a bit of flour and eggs to stretch the batter, and soon she was frying up a batch of her golden, crispy latkes.

The beggar ate the latkes with great relish.

"These are the best potato latkes in all of Russia," he told her.

"Do you really like them?" Tante Golda asked, pouring him a glass of tea from the samovar, a Russian urn used to boil water.

"Do I like them?" the beggar repeated. "They're delicious! And believe me, it's not just because I'm starving! These latkes nourish

Café talk

These latkes are just like my mother used to make — oily on the outside, frozen on the inside.

body and soul. They are a miracle, and one miracle leads to another. You'll see."

When he finished his tea, the beggar thanked her again and said, "God will surely bless you for sharing your latkes with an old beggar."

After the beggar left, Tante Golda took off her apron and climbed up the steps to her sleeping loft above the stove. She was tired but happy—almost as happy as if she had made a Hanukkah party for all her friends and neighbors.

That night, Tante Golda dreamed about latkes—dozens and dozens of them, rising off her griddle, floating out the door, and rolling down the road to the village and into the homes of all her friends and neighbors. When she woke up the next morning, she sighed because her lovely vision had only been a dream after all. She knew there were no potatoes left to make latkes.

But when she got out of bed, she noticed there were two potatoes sitting next to the menorah.

"Risel must have found some extra potatoes after all," she thought to herself. That night she invited Risel over for a batch of her delicious latkes.

The following day, which was the third day of Hanukkah, Tante Golda woke up and saw three potatoes sitting next to the menorah.

"That Gittel is always trying to fool me," she told herself. "She was just pretending she didn't have any potatoes."

And so it went. Each day Tante Golda woke up, there was one more potato sitting next to the menorah. And each night she invited one more guest over for latkes.

Finally, on the last day of Hanukkah, there were eight potatoes sitting next to the menorah, and that evening it was just like it had always been. Eight candles, eight potatoes, eight guests.

Tante Golda stood in front of her black iron stove and cooked batch after batch of her famous latkes.

"These are the most delicious potato latkes in all of Russia," Risel said.

"Not only are they the most delicious latkes," Gittel said, "they're probably the only latkes in all of Russia."

"Tell us, Tante Golda," Hodel asked. "Where did you get the potatoes?"

Moishe winked slyly. "She must be friends with the czar."

"The czar, poor man, has never had the good fortune to taste Tante Golda's latkes," Hodel said.

They all laughed and helped themselves to another latke.

After they were finished eating, Tante Golda turned to her guests and said, "I know this has been a hard winter for all of us, with very few potatoes to go around. I want to thank you for sharing your few potatoes with me."

"But Tante Golda," her guests said. "Much as we wanted to, we weren't able to give you any potatoes. We had none ourselves."

Tante Golda was surprised, but not too surprised. She remembered the beggar's blessing and knew that somehow, as always, God had provided.

When Tante Golda woke up the next morning, she felt sad, as she always did when Hanukkah was over. Perhaps she was even sadder than usual, because now there were no potatoes sitting next to the menorah.

But as Tante Golda got out of bed, she blinked and cried, "It's a miracle!"

Hanukkah Bummer

When a Hanukkah gift comes in a big box and most of it is paper

There, in the corner, was her wooden barrel, filled to the very top with potatoes. She ran over to the barrel and scooped some potatoes into her hands to make sure she wasn't dreaming. This time, she didn't even try to guess where the potatoes came from. She simply thanked God for providing them.

A barrel full of gold couldn't have made Tante Golda any happier. Now she had potatoes to last until spring, with enough left over to share with her friends and neighbors and cook into batch after batch of golden, crispy latkes.

That year, Tante Golda's Hanukkah lasted all winter long.

Joy to the World

by ELLEN FRANKEL

It was a short walk from the synagogue to her home. Sarah hurried through the brisk December air. Above, the last bite of the moon hung temptingly in the sky. Like starved mosquitoes, gusts of powdery snow stung Sarah's cheeks as she shuffled quickly over the icy walks, lugging her heavy package between stiff, mittened hands. By the time she reached her front door, she was chilled to the bone.

"Sarah!" her mother cried when she saw her daughter's pink, chattering face. "I was getting worried; it was so late. You should have called from Hebrew school. I would have come to get you."

"It's okay, Mom. It's not that far," Sarah said, removing her steamed glasses. Her eyes exchanged one blur for another. She couldn't tell her mother why she was late. She couldn't let her know that she had had to wait until everyone was gone from the synagogue building before she could leave. She couldn't let any-one know that she, Sarah Pearl Eisenberg, had brought a Christmas wreath into Temple Shalom!

Earlier that day, Sarah's seventh-grade art class had put the finishing touches on the papier-mâché wreaths they had been working on for a week. Since Sarah always went directly from Franklin Middle School to Hebrew School on Tuesdays, she had had no choice but to bring her wreath with her. So, when the bell had rung, off she'd raced to the synagogue to stash it in the closet behind some old prayer books. No one ever looked in there.

Sarah knew it wasn't right for her, a Jew, to make Christmas decorations, but her whole class had made them. What was she supposed to do, make a scene in front of everyone? Stage a sit-down strike? She was already considered an oddball by all the kids because she stayed out of school for unheard-of Jewish holidays, like Sukkot and Shavuot. Why add to her reputation? Besides, the wreaths were so pretty, with their red satin ribbons and glazed acorns studding the bright green papier-mâché crust. Everyone had loved making them, even Bull Logan and his gang.

"Mom," Sarah said timidly, "look what I made in school." She held up the wreath in one mittened hand.

"What's that?" her mother asked. To Sarah, the question sounded perilously close to an accusation.

"It's a Christmas wreath," she said. "I'm going to hang it up in my room. You know, like a poster or a mobile."

Mrs. Eisenberg frowned, then bit her bottom lip. When she spoke, her voice sounded especially gentle.

"Sarah, darling," she began. The "darling" warned Sarah that trouble was coming. That particular term was usually reserved for bad news.

"You know very well that you can't hang up a Christmas wreath in our house. I've spoken to your principal about this before but it seems I have to go through it again every year with each new teacher." Her voice now betrayed the familiar gritty snarl of annoyance. "When will they learn that Christmas doesn't belong in the public schools?"

"You mean I can't put it up—not even in my own room where nobody but me will see it?" Sarah asked, her wide eyes like little white wreaths with brown centers. "I promise to take it down when my friends come over. I'll hide it in my closet!"

"It's not a question of appearances, sweetheart," her mother said. "It just doesn't belong in our home. We're Jews. Jews don't celebrate Christmas, no matter how popular it is."

Sarah pouted and clutched her wreath. Her mother gently smoothed down her daughter's wet bangs and smiled.

"I know how hard it is for you when so many of your friends celebrate Christmas. I remember crying my eyes out when I was about your age because my parents wouldn't let me have a Christmas tree like my best friend, Betsy Long."

"No kidding!" Sarah cried. "I thought you were always into this Jewish stuff."

"No, not always," her mother said. "Like you, I had first to struggle with how hard it sometimes is to be Jewish in a Christian culture."

"But we learned in school that we live in a *secular* country," Sarah said, proud of the new word she'd just learned from her social studies book. "America was founded on the principle of sep-aration of church and state." Wouldn't Mrs. Lewis be proud of her for applying what she learned in school to real life!

"That's true in theory, Sarah, but in fact, we live in a mostly Christian world," her mother answered. "Look at our downtown, for example. It's as if only Christians lived here. Christmas lights on all the trees, carols piped into the town square, a Christmas parade down Main Street this Sunday. You experience the same sort of pervasive Christmas spirit in your school."

"What's 'pervasive'?" Sarah asked. Her mother was always using wonderful, impressive-sounding words like that. She loved to try them out on her teachers and watch their embarrassment.

"It means 'invading everywhere,'" her mother explained. "In other words, we cannot escape Christmas no matter what we do—especially when there are so few of us living in a small town like ours," she added.

"Why do we have to escape at all?" Sarah asked.

"It's not that we *have* to escape," Mrs. Eisenberg said. "It's just that we have our own beautiful, rich, unique tradition to preserve and enjoy. Our children should not be forced to choose!"

Sarah was beginning to feel guilty about bringing the wreath home. She hadn't realized how upset her mother would get. It wasn't that Sarah was rejecting Judaism; she was just adding to it.

"You can't have it both ways," her mother said as if reading her thoughts. "We don't need to be reduced in spirit, too!"

Sarah abruptly dropped her wreath to the floor like a hot coal. She grabbed her mother's clenched hand. Now she felt awful.

"We have so many beautiful holidays of our own to cele-brate," her mother said gently. "Remember how much fun it was to decorate the sukkah? And think about the dancing and singing you did on Simchat Torah. And there's the seder, too."

Sarah nodded. Her mother was right. She remembered how jealous Deirdre had been when Sarah had shown her the sukkah and explained how they would eat in it for eight days. And the

There's a pencil in your menorah.

Oh my goodness! I must have done my homework with a candle.

seder! Last year they had stayed up until midnight, eating, singing, and giggling from all the wine. Uncle Aaron had been hilariously flat on all the songs, as usual. No, she wouldn't trade any of that for the world.

"I'm sorry, Mom," Sarah said, guiltily. "I just wasn't thinking."

"Nothing to be sorry about, Sarah," her mother reassured her. "You've just had one of your first lessons in trying to live in two worlds. It's possible, but not always easy."

Grinning, she gave Sarah a big hug.

A Miracle for Marci

by MIRIAM RINN

This story is most appropriate for older readers.

Marci pushed aside her English textbook and, stretching her arms high over her head, gazed out the kitchen windows. She had lived in the United States for 11 months now, and in Fairlawn for eight, and the garden in the courtyard of their apartment complex still looked strange to her. It was nothing like the park across the street from their building in Minsk in the Soviet Union. There she had played with her friends and walked with Mama and Papa and Alex after dinner and on Sundays. Here, you never saw anyone walking for pleasure, just people out with their dogs or getting their exercise.

Of course, here they had a car, even though Mama complained that it wouldn't last the winter, and Alex had a chance to go to the best college. It didn't matter that he was Jewish; it only mattered that he was smart. That was why he studied all the time, and why he got to have the small bedroom. Marci had to sleep on the living room couch, but she didn't mind. She could get up very early and watch cartoons on their small TV.

Marci watched as a bulky shape very slowly and cautiously descended the few steps to the sidewalk. Mrs. Gold, the elderly woman who lived in the next apartment, was going out to walk her old dog, Trixie. Marci liked them both; Mrs. Gold was the only person she saw regularly in the courtyard.

Marci glanced quickly at the clock on the wall. It was only four-thirty. She had time to talk to Mrs. Gold before she had to put the soup on to warm. She slid into her coat and gloves and grabbed a scarf on the way out the door. "Mrs. Gold," she called. "Wait. I'll walk with you."

"Why, hello, Masha. How nice to have company!" Mrs. Gold smiled warmly. She wasn't much taller than Marci. "What happened to your beautiful blond braids? You have a new hairdo."

"Mama's girlfriend Vera cut them and gave me a perm." Marci patted her crimped hair. "Do you think I look good?" she asked shyly.

Mrs. Gold put a gloved hand around her shoulder and squeezed. "You look very fashionable, very American."

Marci took a deep, happy breath. "And call me Marci, not Masha."

Mrs. Gold laughed. "What are you doing for Hanukkah, Marci? Any big plans?"

Marci was quiet for a moment. She had heard kids in her class talking about Hanukkah since the beginning of December. They seemed very excited about all the gifts they expected. When she had asked about it at home, Mama had said she thought she remembered some sort of Jewish holiday when she would get money as a gift, but she wasn't sure. Anyway, they were so busy at the discount store where she worked that she didn't have the time or energy to prepare for any holiday. And Marci knew that there was no extra money for presents. Besides, Alex had said that he wasn't interested in Jewish holidays. Being a Jew had already cost him his spot at the Polytechnic Institute in Minsk, and that was quite enough.

Marci looked down at her shoes. "I don't know, Mrs. Gold. What are you supposed to do on Hanukkah?"

They stopped walking to wait for Trixie, who had sat down to rest. "You don't know? *Oy*, what a shame!" Mrs. Gold clucked sympathetically.

"It's different in the Soviet Union," Marci explained. "No one talks about being Jewish. It's as if it's a terrible secret that you can't let anyone know."

"Well, during Hanukkah here," Mrs. Gold explained, "you light candles and you sing songs, and you play with a spinning top called a dreidel. And you eat latkes, potato pancakes, of

Hanukkah Bummer

A Hanukkah party filled with cheek-pinching relatives

course, with applesauce or sour cream. And someone tells the story of what happened to the Maccabees long ago. When I was young, all the children got coins, Hanukkah gelt, but now I think they get presents. I still give my grandchildren money, though."

"It sounds like a party," said Marci, smiling.

They began to walk again, and Mrs. Gold leaned on Marci for support. "That's what people do," Mrs. Gold nodded. "Jewish people, Marci, like you."

Marci imagined being at a party, all the people laughing and singing. Candles would be burning, and Papa and Alex would be trying to beat each other at chess. Marci would read the story of Hanukkah. And everyone there would be happy to be Jewish.

Marci looked seriously at the old woman. "Will you help me, Mrs. Gold, to make a party for my family? A real Hanukkah party?"

"Of course I'll help! It would be my pleasure. Now, let's see—you'll need a menorah and candles, a book that tells the story, a dreidel, and what else . . . ?"

While Mrs. Gold thought, Marci figured quickly in her head. It would cost a lot of money to buy all those things, and she didn't have any money. She certainly couldn't ask Mama or Alex. She wanted the party to be a surprise, a Hanukkah gift for her family. She would have to earn the money somehow.

"I need a job, Mrs. Gold. Could I walk Trixie for you now that it's cold? She likes me." Marci bent down quickly to pet the old dog. She hoped Mrs. Gold wouldn't be angry.

"What a wonderful idea! If you could walk Trixie twice a day, and me once a day, I'd be happy to pay ten dollars a week. How's that?" Mrs. Gold asked.

"Oh, that's too much! Mama will be angry."

"Your mother doesn't have to know. She goes to work around seven, right? You can walk Trixie in the morning after she leaves and when you come home from school. Is it a deal?" Mrs. Gold stuck out her hand.

Marci took it and shook it vigorously, just as people did at home. "It's a deal."

Marci had been walking Trixie and Mrs. Gold for two weeks, and she had saved all of the twenty dollars. She folded the money carefully and put it in her pocket. Today, she and Mrs. Gold were

walking to town to buy all the things they needed for the party. Tomorrow night was the first night of Hanukkah.

"Mrs. Gold, are you ready?" Marcie called through the door impatiently.

The door opened. Mrs. Gold was pinning her hat to her hair. "I'm coming, I'm coming. I can't move as fast as you."

Mrs. Gold locked the door and tucked her arm through Marci's. Slowly, they began the six-block walk to town. "We'll go to that *taleisim gesheft* first—that's a Jewish bookshop. They should have a menorah, candles, and a book about Hanukkah. Then we'll stop at the grocery and get applesauce and sour cream. You said you had potatoes, no?" Mrs. Gold asked.

"Oh yes, we always have potatoes. We eat them every night," Marci answered.

"Good. I have everything I need to make *kichel*, Hanukkah cookies, tomorrow before my grandson picks me up. I even have a cookie cutter shaped like a dreidel. The potato pancakes you made in my apartment for practice were perfect. So we're all set."

When Marci saw the line of shops, her heart began to beat more quickly. It seemed as if it was taking them forever to get to town.

Finally, they stopped in front of a small store with many books in the window. There were silver and brass objects and banners of shiny fabric. Everything was covered with strange markings, letters that Marci didn't recognize. "Come, darling, let's go in," Mrs. Gold said.

Marci felt shy and hesitant. She didn't know what any of the things in the shop window were or what the strange letters meant. She wouldn't know what to ask for, and everyone in the shop would think she was foolish. Maybe she had made a mistake in wanting to give a Hanukkah party. "I don't know, Mrs. Gold. Maybe we should go home. In the Soviet Union, being a Jew only brought trouble."

Mrs. Gold shook her head, suddenly serious. "In America, Marci, we can believe whatever we want, as long as we don't bother other people or keep them from following their own beliefs." Her voice softened. "Now you have a chance to find out how lucky you are to be a part of the Jewish faith. Come, I'll help you find everything you need."

Taking a deep breath of the cold evening air, Marci pulled open the door. Soon, she was deciding between a wooden or brass menorah, a dreidel filled with chocolates that didn't spin very well or one without candy that spun for a full thirty seconds, a blue-and-white or a multicolored "Happy Hanukkah" banner, napkins with pictures of dreidels or a decorated tablecloth made of paper.

"So, young lady," said the man behind the counter. "What will it be?"

Marci clutched the money in her pocket tightly. "I want the wooden menorah, this dreidel without the candy, the tablecloth, and this sign."

"And put in a box of candles," Mrs. Gold added.

The man gathered all the items together and went to the cash register. "That's $16.73."

Marci let out her breath in relief. She had enough for apple-sauce and sour cream, too.

It was when they were leaving the grocery that Marci remembered. "Mrs. Gold, we didn't buy a book, a book that tells about the holiday!"

"*Oy vey!* You're right. And now all the money is gone."

Marci's thoughts raced. Where could she get a book? If they couldn't read about what had happened to the Jews thousands of years ago, it wouldn't be a real Hanukkah party. No one in her family would understand what they were celebrating.

Marci looked at her watch. It was already five-twenty. "We could go to the library, Mrs. Gold. Mama and Papa don't get home until six."

"That's a good idea, Marci, but you go by yourself. I'll never make it that far. I'm already tired, and it's getting cold."

Marci hesitated. She could get to the library and home if she ran all the way. But what about Mrs. Gold? It was dark, and she didn't walk steadily without help. Marci had promised to take Mrs. Gold for a walk each day, and this was today's walk. She couldn't just leave her.

"No, it doesn't matter. Let's go home together."

It seemed to Marci that Mrs. Gold gave a sigh of relief as she took her arm, but Marci was too miserable to care much. Her parents and Alex and Vera would eat the potato pancakes and the

> **Why did Mendel celebrate nine days of Hanukkah?**

> **He had extra candles.**

cookies shaped like dreidels, but they wouldn't know why, and Marci wouldn't be able to explain. She'd never remember what to say when she lit the candle, or the name of the bad king, or when it happened, or where. Her family would have a good time, but it wouldn't be special. It wouldn't be a Hanukkah party.

Marci added the last of the latkes to the tray in the oven and checked the clock. Vera would be arriving soon. Mama and Papa were coming home at the usual time, and Alex had promised to be back from the library.

She looked around to make sure that everything was ready. The menorah with one candle in the middle and one at the end was sitting on top of the TV, with the dreidel right next to it. Marci had tacked the banner over the kitchen door so everyone would be sure to see it. The tablecloth was spread and the table set. Everything looked pretty, but Marci felt as if a stone were sitting on her chest, making it hard to breathe. If only she'd remembered to buy the book, she'd have been glad to use a plain tablecloth.

The knock at the door startled Marci. Could that be Vera already?

When she opened the door, she saw Mrs. Gold holding a plate full of dreidel-shaped cookies and a wrapped package. "I'm sorry I couldn't come earlier, Marci, but my grandson just arrived, and he was bringing me something I needed. Here are the cookies, and here is something special for you. Go on, open it. I have to go in a minute."

Marci took the plate of cookies and placed it on the table. Then she turned her attention to the package. Her first Hanukkah present! What could it be?

Marci untied the ribbon and pulled apart the paper. She gasped when she saw the book. "It's the Hanukkah story! Now I can have a real Hanukkah party."

Mrs. Gold laughed and gave Marci a quick hug. "You can tell me all about it when I come home and we go for our walk."

Just then, Marci's mother came into the living room. "Mashinka, what's this? Something smells delicious, and the table is so fancy."

"We're having a party, Mama, because tonight is a Jewish holiday," Marci said, "and we're Jews."

"Have a wonderful time," Mrs. Gold called back to them as she hurried out the door. "And a happy, happy Hanukkah!"

A Menorah in Tel Aviv

by YA'AKOV

Illustrated by ALEXA GINSBURG

Hey, David! What are you dreaming about?"

David blinked and saw his two friends sitting almost in front of him on the curb. Tel Aviv has some very busy streets, and he hadn't noticed his friends coming.

Joseph was waiting for an answer. At last, David said, "About a menorah for Hanukkah."

What he did not tell the boys was that he was trying to think of a way to ask his father about a menorah. They had thrown out their old metal one when his mother had been housecleaning before the summer. It had been bent and rusty, and the wax drippings from last year's colored candles were still stuck on it. He remembered his father saying, "By next Hanukkah I'll surely have a job and then we will buy a beautiful new menorah."

But only last night, when David was about to remind his father, the dog-eared record book with the family budget was open on the table. David saw his father chewing the end of his pencil. He knew what that meant. There wasn't much work in the building trade these days. David swallowed his words and left the house.

Reuben broke in on his thoughts. "We were just talking about Hanukkah lamps, too," he said.

"Not just about any old menorah," Joseph corrected him. "Think of it, David, they are going to build a giant steel tower right here in the center of Tel Aviv. Maybe like the Eiffel Tower in Paris! And on top will be a mighty Hanukkah lamp. Each light will be a million candlepower! The papers said so today. All of Tel Aviv will be lit!"

David's face lit with sudden joy. "Really?" he cried. "If ... if that's so, we won't have to light a menorah in our homes!"

Joseph roared, "You believe everything, don't you? Didn't you realize that I was joking?"

"And even if they would build a giant-sized Hanukkah lamp, I would still want to light candles of my own," said Reuben. "You ought to see how beautiful our menorah is—it's all hammered silver, decorated with lions and birds, and the candleholders are small and graceful."

"Our Hanukkah lamp uses oil," said Joseph. "You pour a little oil into each holder and light it. And then I ask my father to place the lamp on the windowsill that faces the street, and I go down to the street and look up at our window."

David closed his eyes and said, "I think it would be wonderful to build a giant menorah. When I grow up and become an engineer I will build a huge tower in the center of Tel Aviv. I'll put a great menorah on top of it and each candle will shine with the power of a million candles and nobody will have to light his own menorah at home. On Hanukkah everyone will be amazed, because the night will be as bright as day."

"Say, I've got an idea," Reuben broke in. "Suppose we all go out on the first night of Hanukkah and look at the windows of all the homes to see who has the most beautiful menorah."

"Swell!" cried Joseph.

"Nothing could be more beautiful than a real giant menorah," David said, with a break in his voice.

Finally, he gave in. He could not tell his friends his troubles. Maybe there wouldn't even be a Hanukkah lamp at all in his house this year. And even if there was one, it surely would not be made of hammered silver or burn pure olive oil.

Until the very day before Hanukkah, David had no chance to speak to his father about a menorah. His father still had not found any work. David nibbled his bread and cheese and wondered how to start the conversation. At last, after a small pile of green olive pits had accumulated on his father's plate, he suddenly said, "Dad, what do you think? Would it be possible to build a giant menorah at the top of a tower in the center of Tel Aviv, with a million candlepower for each light?"

"What for?" his father asked. "Where did you get such an idea?"

"If there would only be a menorah like that, everyone would be able to go outside and enjoy it. We wouldn't need our own

Who ate my latkes? Who ate my latkes? Who ate my latkes? Please pass the applesauce

menorah. Then those who could not afford a beautiful menorah of hammered silver would not be"—he finished bravely—"ashamed of their tin menorah."

The father studied his son's face for quite a while. Then he lowered his glance and poked with his fork at the pile of pits in his plate.

"A giant menorah," he said slowly. "No, David, there is no need for it. I understand your thoughts, my son. But the beauty of a menorah is in its small lights. They fill the whole house with a warm glow and they remind every single family of the wonderful Hanukkah story. Best of all is lighting them with your own hands so that you can see their little flames flicker."

"Father, tell me," David interrupted, "what kind of menorah will you buy?"

"Wait and see," answered his father with a steady voice.

David was on edge all day. He kept glancing at the clock on the dresser. When it began to grow dark and the Hanukkah lights started to flicker in the neighboring homes, David's father arose and said, "Bring a stout plank of wood, David, and five potatoes from the pantry." Then he reached into his pocket and opened a penknife.

David soon returned with the board and potatoes.

"Take the knife," said his father, "and split each potato in half. In each half carve a hole big enough to set a candle into. We'll place the halves on the board and we will have a menorah."

David didn't know whether to laugh or cry. He took the knife and started to cut and carve. As he worked with the first potato, it seemed silly to him. With the second one, he tried to cut evenly and smoothly and with the third he enjoyed the idea. A potato menorah! Who ever heard of such a remarkable menorah!

The *shammash* candle stood firm in its holder.

The first candle stood upright, too. And when his father started to sing "Maoz Tzur," the two flames danced and so did their images in the windowpanes.

A few minutes later, David ran toward his friends in the street. Before they could say a word, he cried out, "What a menorah we've got! You never saw anything like it! It's made of potatoes and it's homemade and—"

Hanukkah Bummer

Winning at dreidel when you're playing for raisins

"Potatoes?" said Reuben. "I never heard of a potato menorah."

"Potatoes?" snickered Joseph. "What will you do with your menorah after Hanukkah? Eat it?" He burst into laughter.

David's spirits refused to be dampened.

"Look at the lights," he pointed to his window. In the back of the menorah he saw the blurry image of his father standing behind the lights.

"My father created that menorah," said David proudly. "It shines with a bright and beautiful light. To me, it's the most beautiful menorah in the whole world."

His voice trembled and his wide eyes glistened. Joseph and Reuben looked at him as though they were seeing him for the first time. Then they gazed long and hard at the potato menorah and at the shadow of David's father.

"You know," whispered Reuben, "when you think of it, it is a beautiful menorah."

And Joseph nodded his head in agreement.

How Jeremy Solved the December Problem

by LOIS F. RUBY

I go to a regular, normal school with blacks and whites and Vietnamese kids who are just learning to talk like the rest of us have since we were babies. Two girls in my school read lips and talk with their hands—sign, the teacher calls it, though it looks kind of like they're swatting flies to me. There's a boy in my class named Nainish, and he's got a sister in fifth grade, and they're Indians. Not the feather kind, the *other* kind. But you know what? Out of 322 kids in my whole school—the *whole school*—I'm the only Jewish one, at least until my brother goes to kindergarten next year, if he doesn't flunk nursery school.

Usually it's pretty neat being the only Jewish kid. The other guys are really impressed when I read Hebrew, and I tell them all kinds of stuff about Passover and all, and they ask me questions, and I act like I know all the answers. My mother says, "eight-year-old boys have an answer for everything," and she's right, too, you know.

But every year at that certain time, it gets to be a problem.

People get going on Christmas, making decorations and gift lists and learning those old songs again. Last year my teacher, Ms. Carew, who wears jeans to school sometimes, told us to write a letter promising our parents something we would do for them for Christmas. I wasn't planning to do a thing for my parents for Christmas, but Ms. Carew got me thinking; there's a lot I could do for them for Hanukkah. Like I could polish the menorah, which gets good and dusty from year to year. And I could grate all the potatoes for the latkes, because my mother hates the grating part. (I didn't mention a word about the onions.)

Well, what I wrote was so different that Ms. Carew, who's different from most people herself, asked me to read it right out loud. Boy, everybody started firing questions at me, and I felt like a rabbi or something answering them all.

Mike, this friend of mine, said, " 'Hanukkah' sounds funny."

"That's just because you can't say 'c-h' sounds like I can. I've had more practice, from Hebrew school." Everybody tried it, but when they said their "c-h"s, it sounded like they were coughing really hard. It takes practice, all right.

Then Sam Conroy asked, "But don't you miss Christmas?"

"No. Why should I? But what I'm wondering is, don't you all miss Hanukkah?"

Everyone laughed. Mike said, "Well, we might, if we knew more about it."

That's when I decided to have a Hanukkah party. My mother groaned when I said there were 30 people in my class, so I picked the 25 I liked best, more or less, including Ellie Brewster, who's shorter than practically anybody. But being short sure didn't stop her from gobbling down the latkes. She ate more than Troy Henley, and he eats two tuna fish sandwiches every day for lunch. *Two.*

My whole family decorated the house with blue and white streamers and bright cardboard dreidels and Hebrew letters and a "shalom" poster from Israel Independence Day, and a felt candle box my brother smeared up with glue (I told him it was beautiful, sort of), and, oh, you know, lots of other things. Then we took this

old, old menorah my great-grandfather brought over from Romania, and we put those twisty candles in it. Then we just waited for the doorbell to ring.

The twins, Jeanie and Julie, were first, and wouldn't you know, the first thing they asked was, "Where's your tree?" The twins always do dumb stuff like that. Duke and I could have told you Boonie would be late.

"Did I miss anything?"

"Oh, no, we just got done passing out these dreidels filled with candy. You don't want one, do you?" Boonie wouldn't admit he did, but I tossed him one anyway. I was feeling pretty generous. "Hey, you want to learn some songs?"

"Are they like Christmas songs?" Nainish asked. He didn't know the difference, because he wasn't even a Christian.

"No, they're special Hanukkah songs. Try this one." We started with "I Had a Little Dreidel," which they caught on to pretty fast. I go to school with a bunch of quick learners. When it looked to me like they were getting tired of singing, I said, "Okay, now we're going to play a game. Divide up somehow into four teams. A *nun* team, a *shin* team, a *gimel*—"

"What's a *gimel*?" Bruce Bonini asked.

"It's a Hebrew letter. Like this one, see?" I had to hold the dreidel right up under his nose because he's so nearsighted. "And the fourth team's a *hey* team. Then we spin the dreidel. We'll spin it about 10 times, and whichever team's letter comes up the most, all those people will get prizes. That's not the right way, exactly, but—"

"Prizes? What kind of prizes?"

"I don't know. My dad got them. Maybe it's chocolate gelt; that's money, you know. Maybe something else."

While we were spinning, Adam Jonson asked, "Hey, what is this 'ha-na-ka,' anyway? Is it somebody's birthday?"

"No, nobody's birthday. It's a victory and freedom holiday, kind of like the Fourth of July. You see, there was this mean king named Antiochus."

"'An-tie-o-kiss!' Oh, I love the sound of that," Maureen squealed. Mike just looked at me and rolled his eyes.

"And this king didn't want the Jews to be Jews. He was trying to make them believe things they couldn't, so a real hero named Judah Maccabee got his brothers and some other Jewish soldiers together, and they fought the king's whole army and WON! By then the Greeks had made a mess of the Temple, so the Jewish people started cleaning it up, and they found a little bit of oil to light the menorah. But they figured, such a little bit of oil, it would only last one day, tops. But do you know what happened?"

"What happened? Tell us, tell us!"

"Well, that little bit of oil burned for eight days, like it was a miracle. That's why we light Hanukkah candles for eight days, and that's what those letters on the dreidel stand for—*nun*, *gimel*, *hey*, *shin*—*Nes Gadol Haya Sham*, which means "A great miracle happened there."

They really loved the miracle part. Then my mother brought out about 2,000 crispy, crunchy potato latkes that smelled so unbelievably delicious, and the kids couldn't get enough of them, and when we ran out of sour cream, they all went home. Mike was the last to leave, and guess what he said to me?

"You know, Jeremy, I guess I would miss Hanukkah too!"

What do you know?!

The Hanukkah Blizzard

by HAZEL KRANTZ

Y ou're not bringing that!" Steve Levinson exclaimed to his wife.

Amy looked up from polishing the silver menorah. It was a beautiful menorah, decorated with swirls and silver flowers. Little bells tinkled below each candleholder. "Of course," she said. "The Hanukkah menorah is a family heirloom. My grandmother brought it from Germany. After all, Eleanor is my sister. She has a right to light the menorah too."

Levi made little circles next to his forehead. Ever since his bar

mitzvah, his sister Rachel thought her older brother had become a real jerk. Everyone else was crazy. Only he was the big shot. He had gotten very tall, and his brown hair stood up in ridiculous spikes. Well, next year she would become bat mitzvah and she could be a big shot too.

His mother gave Levi a dirty look. "Aunt Eleanor waits all year for the five of us to spend Hanukkah with her and Uncle Dave and their kids. Good thing this year it comes during winter break."

"Yeah," said Levi. "Skiing. The main event."

"I love Aunt Eleanor's latkes," declared six-year-old Larry. Larry always had his own thoughts.

"We go to Eleanor's in Loveland for the first night of Hanukkah, then up to Breckinridge to ski. That's the plan," said Steve. "And you're going to lug that menorah. Candles, too? Loveland is not the Gobi Desert. They have candles."

"They might not fit."

Finally, Levi agreed to carry the menorah. Loaded down with skis and suitcases, they trailed into La Guardia airport, and checked their baggage. The menorah was carry-on and caused a piercing alarm when it went through security.

The plane to Denver was full of people in ski clothes and a few buttoned-up businesspeople with laptops. As the plane soared west over barren fields, someone began a chant, "Think snow!" and everyone joined in.

"They've had a drought," Steve remarked. "We might end up skiing on mud."

"Bite your tongue," Amy said.

"The weather in Denver is snow!" announced the pilot as the plane zoomed over Kansas fields. The passengers cheered, but the flight attendants looked worried. "Prepare for landing," they said sharply. "No one leave your seat. Buckle up."

The plane descended into swirling snow. Even the passengers began to look nervous. How could the pilot see the runway? The landing was strange. Tires squealed and the plane zigzagged in a crazy way. Finally it stopped and began to taxi, inching its way through the snow. For an hour, it fought its way to the terminal, just a faint blur beyond the huge snowflakes.

Where does a penguin keep its Hanukkah gelt?

In a snow bank.

As the passengers emerged, the airport was eerily silent. All of the gates were empty. The gift shops and newspaper stands in their terminal were closed tightly.

"Ours was the last plane in. All others have been diverted to Kansas City," the pilot told them.

A public address system droned, "All passengers must proceed to the main terminal."

They rode the subway train to the terminal and got their baggage and lugged it into the main terminal. Stranded travelers, walking around upset, were jammed into the terminal. There were people who had planned to fly out, some who were supposed to change planes at Denver, and those who thought they were going skiing. There were people of every description, even from overseas. They grumbled and quarreled over stupid things like seats. As a public address notice repeated, "Do not leave your luggage unattended," people stacked suitcases and skis against the wall. Nervously, Amy clutched her precious menorah. Steve got in touch with Uncle Dave by cell phone. "Can't get out of here," Dave reported. "We've got four feet of snow in our driveway."

Airport employees scurried around. "The food court will remain open. We will supply you with blankets. There will be no planes until tomorrow at least. All highways are snowed in. No ground transportation."

"There goes the bus to Loveland," snorted Levi.

"You had to pray for snow!" his father scolded.

Levi shrugged.

Rachel wished she had something to read. She had already finished her airplane book. Kids were jammed around a television set. People paced, grumbled, and snarled. A few sat down and closed their eyes. Some babies tried to sleep. Others cried. The buttoned-down businesspeople went tap tap on their laptops and for some reason, a large screen in the waiting area started giving golf lessons. The snack shops had lines snaking around, as exhausted food workers tried to serve everyone. The floor was littered with trash.

Outside the big windows there were great blobs of snow twirling and whirling down. No planes were visible, only snow-plows fighting a losing battle against the storm.

It got darker outside. Snowflakes gleamed in reflected light.

"It's Hanukkah, first candle," Steve murmured. He brought out a plastic bag and took out paperback books, magazines, and candy he had bought at the newsstand and handed them out. "Happy Hanukkah."

"I'll bet Aunt Eleanor is making latkes right now," said Larry sadly.

Amy did not say a word. She stood up and carried her menorah to a counter. She put in two candles—the first candle and the *shammash*. She took a ski scarf and put it over her head. She raised the *shammash* candle.

"*Baruch Ata*," she said in ringing tones.

The crowd stopped chattering. Some gaped at her, but others, apparently Jewish, approached the menorah. Soon there was quite a knot of people surrounding the silver menorah, saying the prayer together. An air current swept through, making the little bells below each candleholder tinkle.

"What is this?" a woman in a sari asked a Chinese man.

"It's the feast of lights. The lights of peace," he said.

The woman placed her hands together and bowed reverently.

Their words echoed through Rachel's mind. She had never thought of that. Of course, the eternal light, the *ner tamid*, was the light of peace. That was why it was so important to keep it lit!

As the two candles flickered and the bells chimed, a sense of peacefulness seemed to come across the crowd. They stopped chattering and sat down, on a bench or the floor, quietly gazing at the lights of peace.

"Do you remember the play you did in religious school?" Amy asked Levi and Rachel. "Levi, you were Antiochus."

"Yeah, the bad guy." He snarled, "Heh, heh, heh. What a lovely synagogue. We'll fix that. Bring me pigs and dirt and garbage. We'll mess up your synagogue."

"Oh, no, no," Rachel said. "I'm Mattathias and all who are for the Lord follow me. We must defeat the bad Antiochus."

Silence had fallen on the crowd in the terminal. Children gathered from all over and sat cross-legged in front of the menorah.

Hanukkah Bummer

U.S. MAIL

You send thirty Hanukkah cards and get back two

"Take that and that and that." Little Larry pounded his fists against his brother.

"Oh no. You've got me!" Dramatically, Levi fell to the ground.

"Oh, we must clean up this mess," said Rachel. "Look, the eternal light, the *ner tamid*, the light of peace, is still lit. But there is only a little bit of oil. We must get more. Hurry, hurry."

The healthful latke

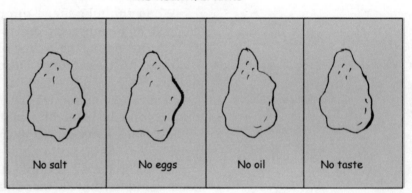

No salt   No eggs   No oil   No taste

"Gotta run to Modin," shouted Levi, miraculously revived. "Come, everybody, run to get the oil."

Kids jumped up and snaked through the terminal in a line, yelling. "Gotta get oil."

"And do you know what?" Amy told the crowd. "For eight days and eight nights, until they were able to get more oil, the little bit of oil burned. The light of peace did not go out."

Larry screwed up his face. "But where are the latkes?"

Steve said, "There's a pancake place. Maybe they can make latkes."

The pancake man had no potatoes and no onions.

"But the Baked Potato Palace has potatoes," Larry pointed out.

"There are plenty of onions at the salad bar."

"Latkes, latkes," was shouted throughout the terminal. Weary food workers brought bowls and plates. The salad man gave onions. The potato man gave potatoes. The pancake man had eggs and batter. The people in the terminal grabbed bowls and mixed, and chopped, and fried.

There were enough latkes for everyone. The potato man ladled out sour cream.

"These are the most delicious latkes I ever had," said Larry dreamily.

Someone started singing, "I had a little dreidel. I made it out of clay." The song echoed throughout the terminal. Chinese people, Indians, Africans, Colorado cowboys, New Yorkers, all singing and when it stopped, snores zizzed throughout the building.

Airport people handed out gray airplane blankets and everyone snuggled up and slept.

When sunlight shone through the windows, the snow had stopped. Bagels appeared and everyone munched contentedly.

Toward noon, the public address system announced, "The highways are clear. Shuttle busses are here. The bus to Loveland is at Door 504."

"That's us," exclaimed Steve. They gathered up their luggage and skis and the menorah and started toward Door 504.

Suddenly, Larry started to cry. "I don't want to leave. I like it here!"

"We'll be back," Levi told him, "on the way home. But now we're going to Aunt Eleanor and Uncle Dave's. We'll tell them all about our airport Hanukkah party."

"I love Aunt Eleanor's latkes," Larry said. "Let's go!"

A Hanukkah Visitor

by MALKA PENN

This is especially good for older readers.

Just after sunset, on the last night of Hanukkah, it began to snow. Snowflakes tumbled out of a gray sky and swirled around the street lamp like white moths dancing around a flame. Roads and sidewalks turned into smooth, satin ribbons. Lights from houses in the distance sparkled like stars through the falling snow.

Margie pressed her nose against the kitchen window and wondered whether her parents would be later than usual. Even on a clear night they didn't get home from their store until nine-thirty or ten o'clock.

She drew away from the window and struck a match to light the shammash candle. Then she repeated the blessing she had said every night for the past week.

"*Baruch Ata Adonai, Eloheinu Melekh ha-olam, asher kideshanu bemitzvotav vetzivanu le-hadlik ner shel Hanukkah.* Blessed are You, Lord our God, Ruler of the universe, who has sanctified us with Your commandments and has commanded us to kindle the Hanukkah lights."

She used the *shammash* to light the eight Hanukkah candles that stood in a row in the brass menorah on the windowsill. One by one, their flames were reflected in the window, so that it seemed as though there were two menorahs burning brightly. She wished her parents could see the Hanukkah lights, but she knew the candles would burn out before they got home.

Then she switched on all the electric lights, even the ones over the sink and the stove, and began to prepare her supper—a cheese sandwich on toast, two pickles, and a glass of soda.

As she sat down at the table to eat, a gust of wind rattled the window and made the candle flames flicker. All during supper, the wind grew louder. Once or twice, the electric lights, as well as the candles, flickered. Margie tried to drown out the noise of the wind by turning on the radio, but the static was louder than the music and she flipped it off again.

Another gust of wind made the candles dance, and then, without warning, all the electric lights went out. Only the Hanukkah candles saved the room from total darkness.

Margie ran to the window and looked outside. There were no lights anywhere—not from the street lamp, not from the houses in the distance.

"It's quite dark in here, isn't it?" a voice said.

Margie spun around. Standing by the table, less than five feet away from her, was a girl about her own age, dressed in a long skirt and boots, with a shawl over her blouse and a scarf tied around her head.

"Who . . . who are you? How did you get in here?" Margie was startled to see the girl, but she wasn't frightened. There was something familiar about the smiling, friendly face in front of her.

The girl seemed amused by Margie's questions. "My name's Malke, of course. And I didn't *get* in here. I live here."

Margie looked around the room. It had changed. In place of the electric range, there was a black iron wood-burning stove. Where the radio had sat on the counter, a samovar, a Russian urn used to boil water, now stood in a wooden cupboard. A rough, planked table had replaced the modern dining set in the center of the room.

The only thing that remained the same was the brass menorah on the windowsill. Malke walked over to it and picked it up. She carried it to the wooden table and set it down.

"There. That should give us more light." She began to stir a large pot on the stove. "The borscht should be ready soon. I thought it would be good on a cold, snowy night like tonight."

"Where, where are your parents?" Margie asked.

"Oh, Mama is helping a neighbor who's having a baby. She's the midwife, you know. And Papa is staying late at the synagogue tonight, cleaning up. He's the caretaker there. So it's just me—and you," she added with a twinkle in her eye. She glanced at the menorah on the table. The candles had burned about a third of the way down. "I wish they were able to see the Hanukkah lights. I love it on the last night when all the candles are lit."

"Yes, me too," Margie agreed. She was still bewildered by the strange surroundings and by the girl who had come out of the dark, snowy night, but she also felt comforted by her new companion. At least, she thought to herself, she wasn't alone on this last night of Hanukkah.

Malke ladled out two bowls of steaming borscht and set them on the table. She motioned Margie to sit down and eat.

"Tell me what you think of the borscht."

Margie sat down hesitantly and blew at a tablespoon of the hot soup. Two red drops of borscht splashed on the sleeve of her blouse.

"That's all right," Malke said. "Go ahead, taste it," she urged.

Malke smiled. She leaned toward Margie and lowered her voice as if she were telling her a secret. "I put three cloves in it. I learned that trick from my grandmother."

"My grandmother's name was Malke," Margie said, sipping the soup. "I was named after her."

"Oh, so you're Malke, too?"

"Well, my Hebrew name is Malke. My English name is Margie, which is short for Marjorie."

"Margie." Malke repeated the name and nodded her head approvingly.

The girls finished their bowls of soup. By that time the candles had burned more than halfway down. Little pools of melted wax glistened on the tops of the candles. For a while, the girls sat quietly watching the candles grow smaller. Finally, Malke broke the silence.

"This menorah belonged to my grandmother," she said. "One day my mother will hand it down to me and then I'll hand it down to my daughter and she'll hand it down to hers."

"Our menorah has been handed down that way, too," Margie said. She stared at Malke and suddenly realized why her face seemed so familiar. There was a picture in the family album of Margie's grandmother when she was young. She, too, wore a scarf over her head and had a twinkle in her eye, like Malke's.

"I never met my grandmother," Margie said. "She died before I was born, but my mother has told me stories about her. Before she came to America, she lived in a little house in Russia, just like this one." She looked around the room, still amazed at what she saw.

"Maybe you'll tell your daughter stories about her—and about me, too," Malke smiled. She looked at the menorah. The candles had burned almost all the way down. "It's time to put the menorah back on the windowsill," she said, handing it to Margie.

"We can leave it on the table."

"Please. Put it on the windowsill," Malke insisted. There were tears in her eyes, but the twinkle was still there, too.

Margie stared at Malke for a moment before she took the menorah and carried it across the room. As she set it down on the windowsill, the candles sputtered and then went out completely. But exactly at that moment, light filled the room. The electricity had come back on.

"Malke, the lights!" Margie spun around, just as she had done earlier that evening.

This time, however, Malke was gone. Gone, too, were the black iron stove, the samovar, and the planked table. Everything was exactly the way it had been before the lights had gone out.

Had it all been a dream? Margie wondered. Had she only imagined Malke?

She looked down at her blouse. Two faded red spots stained her sleeve where the borscht had spilled.

No, Malke was real, Margie thought to herself. Maybe not in this time or place, but she existed somewhere, and on that last night of Hanukkah, the two of them had come together to share the beauty of the Hanukkah lights.

The Hanukkah Gift

by MAX ROBIN

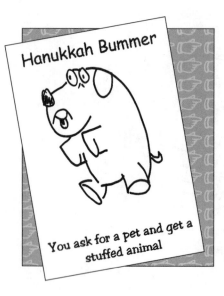

Hanukkah Bummer

You ask for a pet and get a stuffed animal

Snow fell early that year, and as it fell, little children, their noses pressed against the window panes, chanted, "Uncle *Shneyer* is coming! Uncle Snowman is coming!" The earth was covered with a wide, white blanket, and children, whose memory is young, forgot that the earth was ever green. Hanukkah was in the air.

Reb Avrum, the visiting teacher, was the first to refer to it. He came to the Zelnicks one evening, his nose like a carrot, tears brimming his eyes. A skeleton inside his ancient yellow coat, he stood rubbing his hands together over the live stove.

"A glass of tea, maybe?" asked Mrs. Zelnick.

"A glass of tea has never done one any harm—" But it was understood that something with the tea might do one good. The expression on the face of Reb Avrum mellowed as he patiently went about making himself at home. He sipped his tea, then made a feast of it by dunking a section of his crisp cinnamon cookie into the tea.

The teacher was in no hurry to begin the lesson he had come to give the boy, Mendele. He spoke about the terrible winter, the soaring prices of fuel and flour. And as he scraped the last deposit of pasty cookie out of the bottom of the glass, he described a string of misfortunes that had befallen his home, all caused by poverty. And then—

"Time doesn't stand still," he observed wistfully. On a note of cheer, he announced, "Hanukkah is on its way—it is now on just the other side of the threshold."

To Mrs. Zelnick's inevitable question about the first candle, the teacher's deliberate reply was, "The first candle this year will be blessed on Thursday,"—and, more emphatically—"Yes, this coming Thursday!"

Mendele had often heard his mother say that "troubles speak." And his gaunt instructor had more than his share of them, judging by his remarks. It was a temptation to follow Reb Avrum home and see what it was like there. One day he had seen him with a boy who was obviously his son. As he turned to look after them, Mendele noticed that the boy, who was not much older than Mendele himself, walked barefoot. It was summer then. What was his teacher's son doing now, in the winter? Hanukkah time, too!

The day was bleak, the sun was hidden, leaving the earth to the mercy of the winter. In the evening, as he was being put to bed, Mendele asked, "Mama, when will you sew our Hanukkah pouches?"

"Yes, Mama, when?" Mendele's sisters, Sarah and Bessie, chimed in after him. "It's time!"

And mother, tucking the edge of the quilt around the shoulders of her children, answered, "Tomorrow I will sit down and sew the best Hanukkah pouches you ever had."

The children lay awake. From the kitchen the light fell in ornamental designs on the ceiling and floor. Father and Mother were there, talking in whispers. Soon the world would light up with Hanukkah lamps.

Their mother kept her promise and turned out three beautiful pouches for her three beautiful children—red and yellow for the girls, a green one for the boy. They could be opened or closed by loosening or tightening the string at the top. And their purpose, of course, was to hold the Hanukkah gelt that the children had begun to collect.

Mother and Father were first with their gift of a handsome deposit. Aunt Esther came, smelling of butter and cream, then Uncle Hersh-Behr dropped in from out of town.

The money was counted repeatedly, to compare savings. The children slept with their pouches suspended from their necks. They dangled and jingled their treasures.

Reb Avrum did not discontinue his visits during the holiday season. Mrs. Zelnick served him a mammoth latke with his tea, and then she fried him another. Mendele watched his tutor eat with a sense of pleasure.

What's the difference between a candle and a red tablecloth?

You don't know! Then don't come to my house on Hanukkah.

"Mrs. Zelnick," said Reb Avrum, "your latkes are the best, the biggest in town. May your hands continue to make them 'til the age of a hundred and twenty. If it's all the same to you, I'll take the second latke home. Let my family taste it, too."

Thereupon, Mrs. Zelnick fried two more latkes for Reb Avrum to take home. These she wrapped in a towel.

Mendele could have hugged his mother for her thoughtfulness. He had never told her about his teacher's son—the skinny boy with sharp eyes, hollow cheeks, and no shoes.

The purses of the Zelnick children grew until they swelled at the chest. Thank God for a holiday like Hanukkah—its heroes, its customs, its spirit of cheer, which light up the winter. The dancing eyes of the young Zelnicks reflected the triumphant glow of the Hanukkah lamp, reflected the glory of a people.

"What are you going to do with your Hanukkah money this year?" Mr. Zelnick asked at the dinner table one evening with a twinkle of amusement in his eyes.

Mendele wasn't anxious to answer, and his sisters followed his lead. But the subject, having been introduced by their father, flared into a free-for-all discussion when the children found themselves alone later in the evening. There was no doubt about what the girls intended to do with their savings. One had set her mind on a sturdy pair of boots designed to buck the harshest weather, while the younger girl had firmly fixed her heart on the prettiest little muff with fancy white trimming.

The boy, who had only pretended to participate up to this point, was now ready to speak up in earnest. "I know what I'm going to do with my Hanukkah money!" Mendele announced. "Our teacher is poor—he lives at the edge of the town. I'll bet he uses scooped-out potatoes for a Hanukkah lamp! I know his son Ephraim doesn't even own a pair of shoes. Maybe we could all give him our Hanukkah gelt."

The girls were silent. But Mendele thought it would be a shame to spend all their money—an assortment of so many precious coins, given to them by such nice people—in exchange for things they didn't need! He would not do it—even if the girls did!

Finally Sarah asked, "Why should we listen to you? Why can't we ask Mother?"

How could Mendele object—especially when their mother, attracted by the tumult of their rising voices, appeared on the scene? The children explained their discussion to her. Mr. Zelnick, too, joined his family in the children's cozy bed-room.

"How much of a bank do you have in your purses?" Father asked.

"Two-ninety!" The boy had his answer ready. The girls had two-twenty each.

"That's a lot of money!" Their father nodded thrice in appreciation. "I'm not going to try to add it all up. So I'll tell you what we'll do."

The darkness concealed the faces of the children tensed with suspense, while their parents conferred outside. When they returned it was Mother who announced the verdict.

"Your father and I have decided to take half of what you have; we'll make up the other half and let you present the full amount to Reb Avrum."

There were exclamations of delight from the three young Zelnicks. Each was eager to present the belated Hanukkah gift to the teacher and his son Ephraim. Why not present it all together, with Mendele as spokesman?

Later that night, Mr. Zelnick stood at the door of his children's room and listened. Not a sound inside. He tiptoed in.

Then Father stopped at every bed, bent over, and planted a kiss on the head of each child.

A Hanukkah Discovery

by MURIAL GERELICK

Danny was crying, and Danny hardly ever cried. He was pretty brave about most things. He never cried about a lost baseball game or a scraped knee. But this was different. Danny had a prob-lem, and there was no way out. In less than four hours the whole family would gather around the shining Hanukkah menorah. Ten-year-old Danny would light the *shammash* candle. Susie, who was eight, would take the *shammash* and light her candle for the first night of Hanukkah. Four-year-old Billy would just jump up and down with excitement. Dad would chant the blessings and then the whole family would sing "Maoz Tzur."

Hanukkah Bummer

Being the third candle
in the Hanukkah play

Danny could picture just how it would be. After the singing there would be an exchange of gifts. Everybody, even baby Billy, would have a gift to give every other member of the family. This year, though, it would be different. This year no one would get a present from Danny. The very thought prompted another flood of tears, and Danny fell back on his bed, covering his sobs with his pillow.

Through the pillow Danny heard Mother calling, "Danny, this is the third time I've called you. Please come down. I need some more potatoes to make the latkes for tonight and I want you to go to the grocery store."

Mother didn't even look at him when he brushed by her at the kitchen sink. "Take the money that's on the table. Get five pounds of potatoes and hurry getting home."

Danny didn't answer because he felt the tears coming again and he didn't want Mom to know. Not yet. Time enough tonight for her to find out that he had spent or lost all the money he should have saved from his allowance each week to buy gifts for the family. He picked up the money and ran from the room.

Danny blinked at the sun as he hopped on his bike. After all the hot tears, the cold wind on his cheeks felt good. Suddenly, he saw his best friend Tommy up ahead. Tommy waved as the bike whizzed by, and Danny screeched to a stop. In a flash he was standing in front of his friend.

"Tommy, I'm in real trouble," Danny told his friend. He poured out all his sorrows while Tommy bent a sympathetic ear. He let out a deep sigh as he finished. "So you see," he said, "I *gotta* get the money. If you'll just lend me some, I'll do your homework, or help with your chores, or anything you ask. And I'll pay you back as soon as I can. Honest I will."

Tommy dug deep in his pockets. "Gee, Dan, that's rough. You need a bigger miracle than the Maccabees and their flask of oil to get you out of this. All I've got is seventeen cents, but you can have it if it will help."

"Thanks, Tom. I'll never forget you for this."

On his bike again, Danny felt his mind racing wildly. *Maybe there's still a chance*, he thought. *As soon as I get home I'll search the basement for the pennies I've dropped there from time to time. Maybe I can even find the billfold I lost. I know there's some money in that.*

There's still three hours left. Still time to find the money and buy gifts for everyone.

Danny loved the clutter of the basement, especially the pile of junk in the corner. His mother was forever nagging to get the basement cleared of all the junk, but to Danny it was more than just junk—old comics to be reread on rainy days; dented Ping-Pong balls, guns, and marbles; games lacking some parts and some parts lacking a game. Danny started to search for the missing coins in the treasures of the junk pile.

He found so many things he'd almost forgotten about. There was Susie's favorite doll. The arm had come loose and he had promised his sister he would fix it. He dug deeper in the pile. Mom's right, he thought. There is a lot of junk here we don't need. Someday I will get it all cleaned out. Then he found a nickel in his old baseball mitt. The jingle of the coins in his pocket gave him the inspiration to go on with the search.

The sight of Billy's wagon near the bottom of the pile bothered Danny a little. He'd promised to paint it last summer and it was still here. Three pennies turned up in an old pencil box. Danny dug faster. Time was running out and there was still so much to do.

Mother's voice was frantic. "I just don't know where he can be. He's not in his room and I've called all his friends. No one has seen him since early afternoon. What could have happened to him?"

Father tried desperately to find the answer. "I thought he would come running when he saw it was time to light the menorah. Are you sure you've looked everywhere? The garage? The basement?"

"The basement," cried Susie. "We didn't look there!" In an instant four pairs of anxious feet headed for the basement stairs.

Danny was startled at the sound of the footsteps. A quick glance at his watch told the story. He had forgotten the time. Hanukkah was here and he had gifts for no one.

Then they were there, the four of them standing in silent amazement staring at him. Finally Billy broke the silence. "My

wagon! You painted my wagon and it's red and shiny! Is it dry yet? Can I ride it? Can I? Can I?"

Before anyone could answer, Susie danced by, hugging the doll she had picked up from the table. "Oh, thank you, Danny. You fixed her. Pretty Prissy, my most favorite doll. Now her arm is as good as new. What a wonderful Hanukkah surprise!"

Danny felt the tears coming again—happy tears brought on by the sight of the happy smiles of his family, Susie hugging her doll, Billy patting his wagon, Dad admiring the neatness of the cleaned-out tool chest, Mom beaming at the clean basement. Through his tears, Danny told the whole story. "I didn't plan it this way at all," he finished. "It just sort of happened."

Mother smiled. "I don't think it 'just happened.' Perhaps you didn't plan it that way, but the Maccabees didn't plan on the flask of oil lasting eight days, either. Yet, we have always considered that story a wonderful miracle. Do you know why, Danny? Because that little flask of oil has taught generations of people the importance of freedom. What happened here tonight may not be a miracle, but because it happened, all of us have made another important Hanukkah discovery. The most precious gift of all is what we give of ourselves."

In the silence that followed, the whole family thought about Mother's words: *The most precious gift of all is what we give of ourselves.* And then the silence was broken by little Billy, who couldn't quite understand what was going on. Hanukkah laughter filled the room as Billy asked soberly, "We gonna spend all of Hanukkah just thinking in the basement? Or are we gonna go upstairs and eat some latkes?"

The Hanukkah of Great-Uncle Otto

by MYRON LEVOY

illustrated by DONNA RUFF

Joshua knew that Hanukkah was coming. The holiday was in the bare trees, their few remaining leaves shaking like candle flames. It was in the first thin snow, covering the ground like fine lace. But most of all, it was in his Great-Uncle Otto.

"Joshua," Great-Uncle Otto said in his booming voice of old Europe, "Hanukkah is flying toward us like a winter bird, a bird with shining wings spread like a great candelabrum. I can hear it from far off just as I did when I was a little boy in Europe, in Germany. The same winter bird—Hanukkah."

As he spoke, Great-Uncle Otto reached for his tea kettle, but slowly, for his arms were crippled with arthritis and his hands were as stiff as the frozen earth. Seeing him struggle, Joshua leaped up and put the battered kettle on the hot plate. And since his great-uncle always liked something sweet with his tea, Joshua searched in a drawer of the big oak desk for the bag of candy.

Around them in the shop was the clutter of many years: copper pipes like streaks of lightning, wood in strips and blocks, cast-iron machinery too heavy to move and all the old ovens, refrigerators, lawn mowers, chairs, and tables that customers had left for repairs and had never taken back. Joshua and his friends had often used this great jungle of discarded wreckage for imaginary space missions and undersea battles. And at the end of their games, there was always something for them: paper cups with soda or milk or juice. Uncle Otto always had paper cups for everyone—the children, the customers, the mail carrier, the rent collector, everyone.

But now there were no more customers, for Great-Uncle Otto could no longer hold the repair tools in his stiff, trembling hands. He couldn't even hold his cup without spilling tea all over the desk. So he let Joshua help him with his tea every afternoon, but only when they were alone.

At home, Uncle Otto dropped food at the table and wouldn't let anyone help him. He would tell Joshua's mother, "I'm not a cripple! I'm not a baby!"

"He's too proud, that's what he is," Joshua's mother would say when Otto wasn't there. "Too proud to let anyone do anything for him."

At home, Uncle Otto was an old man, a sad, quiet man, and not a great-uncle at all.

But in his shop, in his chair by the desk, he could still be a tower of strength, a teller of stories, a great-uncle wiser than any book. And so he went to his shop each day, saying, "In case a customer comes, I can still repair anything." But Joshua knew that Great-Uncle Otto really went to his shop to become himself again.

Uncle Otto waved his arms slowly and said, "Hanukkah is beating its wings nearer and nearer. Yes, it is." Joshua watched his thin white hair float above his head as he nodded again and again. "Hanukkah is almost here."

"Uncle Otto? Could you tell me a Hanukkah story?" asked Joshua. "A real long one?"

"I'll tell you a short one," said Uncle Otto, "but a true one. It happened—let me see—seventy-five years ago across the ocean in Germany, when times were happy, long before Hitler came with his ugly, lunatic hate. I was a little boy then, as young as you, Joshua. It was the first night of Hanukkah—wait! The hot plate is on high; the teapot will burst—the first night, and I was supposed to put the menorah on the table and light the *shammash*, the center candle, just as you do now. Ah, that menorah. It was old even then. It was my father's father's menorah. Imagine!"

As he lowered the heat under the teapot, Joshua said, "It must be two-hundred years old by now."

"At least," his great-uncle said. "So I took the menorah and—

who could believe it—I dropped it. It slipped, I tripped, who knows. The delicate arms were bent out of shape, and I stood there crying because I was afraid of what my father would do. Fathers then weren't like fathers now. They were strict. Serious. Stern. They loved us—oh, yes—but with a strict, serious, stern love. So there I was, scared as if I burned down the house. And what did my father do? Did he hit me with a belt? Did he?"

"Yes!" said Joshua decisively.

"He didn't!" Great-Uncle Otto boomed. "Strict, serious, stern, but he didn't. No. He took the menorah and bent the arms this way, that way, and little by little they were almost straight. And he asked me why I was crying like a broken *halil*, like a broken reed flute. The menorah was damaged, yes. But that wasn't so important. The meaning of the menorah, that was important. That was valuable. And that could never be damaged. And my father asked me, while I was still shaking, what I thought the menorah meant. So I'll ask you. What do you think?"

Joshua hesitated, just as he did at school, afraid of making a mistake and looking foolish. In class, he always sat quietly, never answering if he could help it. "The quiet one," his mother called him.

"It's . . . it's about the Jewish people," said Joshua, "and how they fought to get their temple back from the enemy, King Antiochus. And when they won, they lit the menorah in the Temple. There was only enough oil for one day, but it burned for eight days, and that's why we light one candle on the first night of Hanukkah, and two candles on the second night, and so on, up to eight. But you know, I wish we could light all eight candles every night."

"Ah!" said Great-Uncle Otto. "But that's it! One candle, then two, then three. That's where the real meaning hides, my father said. The menorah tells us how freedom spreads, how faith spreads, how kindness spreads. The servant candle in the center of the menorah—the *shammash*, the 'sexton'—gives its light to another candle and another, until that one little light becomes many lights, becomes a beacon, a festival, a feast of lights. That's what my father said to me, and that's what can never be lost or damaged, no matter what happens to the menorah. For me, this memory has become a true part of the Hanukkah story. Yes. Yes. We all have our special memories. Someday you'll have yours, too. And the teapot's boiling over!"

As Joshua raised the kettle off the hot plate and prepared a cup of tea, he wondered what special memory he would ever have about Hanukkah. He carefully raised the cup to Great-Uncle

Otto's lips, and Otto put his shaking hands over Joshua's hands as if he, too, were holding the cup.

"Ahh, that's good hot tea," said Great-Uncle Otto, "prepared by my expert." He took a long sip, then a nibble of halvah, and gave a deep sigh. After a moment he said, "Hanukkah is coming, yes, and this beautiful holiday should be happy. But not for me. No. No. I'm completely useless now. Your mother and father have to help me with everything." He pushed back his chair abruptly and stared out the window at the snow. There was a long moment of silence.

Joshua tried to think of something cheerful to say. Great-Uncle Otto had never been like this in his shop before. Maybe at home, but not here. He remembered how his great-uncle had cheered him up last year when his dog, Feller, had finally died of old age. But now Uncle Otto seemed just as old and sad and helpless as Feller had been.

"Uncle Otto," Joshua said softly, trying to tiptoe around the edge of his sadness, "you aren't useless at all. You can do all kinds of things. If you want, you can help me light the *shammash* for Hanukkah." He carefully lifted the teacup again.

"Ummm," Uncle Otto murmured, pushing the cup aside. He stared out the window once more.

"You can light all the candles," said Joshua, trying harder to cheer him up. "Dad wouldn't mind. Okay?"

"Aha, Joshua," Great-Uncle Otto said sadly. "That's exactly it. Your father wouldn't mind this. Your mother wouldn't mind that. I do nothing for them anymore. Nothing. They feed me. They clothe me. They take me to the store, to the doctor, to the relatives, everywhere. . . . I'm just an old man who can't do anything for anyone anymore. I can't even hold my own teacup."

"But . . . but you tell such good stories," said Joshua hopefully.

"Stories? Yes. Stories I have plenty. But you can't eat stories, You can't wear stories. No. Enough stories. I want to do something for your father and mother. But what?" He paused and rubbed his head with a shaking hand. "Maybe I can make them something, as a gift for all their goodness. A gift from me to them. And . . . I think I know exactly what it will be. I think I know. Yes. I already know."

Joshua couldn't wait. "What is it? Uncle Otto? Please? Huh? What?"

"A Hanukkah menorah. I want to make a menorah for them."

But . . ." Joshua hesitated. Should he say it? Would it make him sad again? "But we . . . we have one already, Uncle Otto."

"Oh, yes, yes. A very nice menorah. Modern. Streamlined. No decorations. No curves or bends. But I'm going to make a different kind of menorah. In my menorah, the stems for the candles will twist like flowers on a vine, like that menorah I told you about, the menorah of my childhood. When we escaped from Germany, from Hitler, we couldn't take anything. Not our clothes, not our dishes, nothing. Not even my father's menorah. Thank God I was able to come to your parents here in America. . . . Yes, I'm going

Hanukkah Bummer

When you tip the applesauce jar a little and a lot comes out.

to try to make that menorah come back to life. For your father and mother to give to you some-day, and then for you to give to your children someday. That will be my gift. But I need your help. My hands are only good for waving in the air. These stiff, stupid hands. Will you help me?"

"Yes!" cried Joshua. It was wonderful. Great-Uncle Otto seemed happy again, happier than he'd been for months.

"All right," said Uncle Otto. "Tomorrow. Tomorrow we begin. Tomorrow is menorah day. But remember, it's a secret. It's our secret until the first night of Hanukkah."

Joshua raced home, the snow swirling in streaks like Great-Uncle Otto's thin white hair. He couldn't wait to see his father and mother and not tell them the secret, to know something that his parents definitely didn't know.

"So," said his mother as Joshua stomped his feet and took off his boots. "What have you been doing all afternoon?"

"Nothing."

"Have you been by Uncle Otto's shop?" she asked

"Uh . . . sure, like always."

"How is he? Did you make him some tea?"

"Sure," said Joshua.

"Why aren't you looking at me? Why are you looking down?" asked his mother. "That means trouble. I can tell every time. What's going on? Is something wrong with Uncle Otto?"

"No, nothing, Mom."

"Hmmm. Well, everything comes out in the end," said his mother. "But if you are planning some kind of trick or something, forget it. Remember, Hanukkah is coming, so I have to prepare for all the relatives and I don't have time for your craziness. And don't drive Uncle Otto crazy either."

Joshua felt that he would explode with the secret. He started to laugh, but quickly turned the laugh into a cough. It was really hard, harder than he'd ever thought, to keep a secret, secret.

The next day, after school, Joshua went directly to Great-Uncle

Otto's shop. The sun was out, the snow was melting, and it was yellow-orange autumn again. Uncle Otto was sitting in the window, waiting for him. His face seemed to glow. Joshua almost danced at the sight of his great-uncle looking so eager.

"So, Joshua," Otto said, his voice booming louder than ever, "today is the day we begin. Look, I've cleared a worktable. See all those tubes and wood. That's our menorah."

But it couldn't be. How could those lengths of copper pipe and those blocks of wood ever become a delicate nine-stemmed menorah? It would be easier to turn a stone into a statue.

"Now listen closely," said Great-Uncle Otto. "You have to become my hands. My fingers. We have to cut this copper tube with this pipe cutter. You tighten the tube in the vise like so. Yes, yes. Good, Joshua. And now you pick up the pipe cutter and hold it . . . the other way. . .Yes, good. Now you fit it in place. Yes. Now turn it. Turn it more . . . Good, good. Very, very good"

Joshua struggled to hold the tool correctly, the way he'd seen his great-uncle hold it before he'd become so crippled. But Joshua's fingers felt unsteady and clumsy, and sometimes his hand moved one way while the tool moved another. He worked all afternoon, cutting and filing the tubing into shapes and sizes to fit the menorah: long tubes to curve outward for the end candles and straighter tubes toward the center. Little by little, the tool and his hands began moving smoothly, together.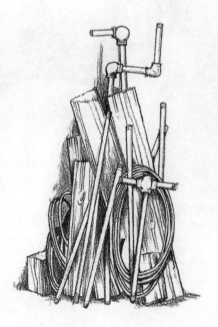

Every so often, as he worked, Joshua studied his great-uncle. He looked happy! Happy! No longer the way Joshua's dog, Feller, had looked before he'd died.

"Yes! Yes!" said Great-Uncle Otto. "It's beginning to become my father's father's menorah. That beautiful menorah! . . . What memories! . . . When I was a boy in Europe, we would put it in the window of our old apartment three flights up. And when it was lit, after the blessings had been said, my cousin and I would run down into the street to see it from below. My father always called, 'No,' but we went anyway. We were mischievous, yes. I remember how it was on the eighth night, with all the candles blazing. I would look up at our window, and there was my bird of Hanukkah with wings of fire, my beautiful shining Hanukkah bird above that narrow street. I remember, it was so cold my cousin and I had to run back upstairs to all the warm smells and the food and everybody laughing."

"Uncle Otto?" asked Joshua, "was your cousin ever at our house?"

"No . . . no. He didn't come to America. He couldn't escape from Hitler in time. Even with your father's help . . . ah, well . . . No sad memories. No . . . In those early days, when we were young, I only saw my cousin once a year, on Hanukkah. He lived far away. I remember he and I would be very mischievous sometimes."

"Like me," said Joshua as he filed a copper tube.

"Ah! Worse! Once we took apart an old clock and made dreidels from some of the big gears on their pivots. We didn't know that the clock was still working, was still good. We painted little colored dots on the gears and as we spun them, the dots became circles, one inside the other, blue, green, red, yellow. The next thing I knew, my father was standing there looking at us very

sternly. The clock was wrecked. My mother tried to convince him that we had made something just as beautiful and important as the clock. Suddenly I had an idea. I started to spin the clock-dreidels on the table top to show him. And what do you think? After a little while, my father tried spinning one, too. When it jumped off the table, he laughed out loud. Soon, everyone was spinning them, seeing who could make them spin the longest . . . Yes . . . yes . . . We were happy in those old days. But then I grew up. Time passed. And Hitler came with his speeches, his storm troopers, his hate. We were afraid to put a menorah in the window anymore. And soon after that, the real horrors began . . . Well, well . . . Enough. Enough stories for today. And enough work for today, too. And this hard work deserves a rest. Let's have some tea and crackers."

Every afternoon that week, Joshua went to the repair shop to work on the menorah. Great-Uncle Otto selected a wooden block with a swirling grain and told Joshua how to cut and chisel and drill the block until it became a delicate boat-shaped base to hold the nine copper stems of the menorah in place. And for each stem, Uncle Otto showed him how to fasten a little cup to hold the candle, a cup for every night of Hanukkah.

"So. The first branch is done," said Great-Uncle Otto. "And the second, and the third. See, we have three nights already. It reminds me of something amazing that happened once on the third night of Hanukkah . . . Yes . . ."

"Tell me," said Joshua, as he started to work on the little cup for the fourth candle.

"So long ago . . . as if it happened yesterday. In the old days, we were very poor. We lived in one of the oldest parts of the town. The houses were so old that they seemed to lean on each other to hold each other up. Sometimes at night I'd wake up and touch the wall behind my bed to make sure it was still there. . . . What was I saying?"

"The third night of Hanukkah," Joshua reminded him.

"Ah, yes. That night, just after the lights had been lit, the *shammash* and three more, our apartment started to shake. The plates and cups jumped on the shelves, and some of them shattered on the floor. We thought it was an earthquake. My father took the menorah in one hand and put his free arm around my mother and me, and we all stood in the corner of the room. I felt safe with my father so close. Through all this, my father managed to recite the blessings. And suddenly the shaking stopped.

"The next morning, when we looked outside, we saw that the house next door had sunk almost a foot and was pushing right up against our building. It had collapsed from old age, everybody said. But why only that house? Nobody really knew. It was so badly damaged, it had to be taken down, stone by stone. For years after, my mother would say that we'd all been spared, everyone, because my father had been so observant, saying the blessings like that. So religious. Yes, I have memories . . . so many memories . . ."

Slowly, day by day, the menorah on the worktable grew and blossomed like a young tree sending out branches. And as Joshua worked and listened to the tales of Hanukkahs long past, the

Hanukkah Bummer

When you meet your cousin at a party and can't remember his name

menorah in his hands seemed almost to come alive, as if he were holding the very same menorah as the one in the stories.

Yet something was wrong. Great-Uncle Otto shook his head again and again but said nothing. That Friday, during a long afternoon of work, he leaned back and studied the menorah—carefully with one eye shut.

"It's a good menorah," he said. "A nice menorah. But . . ." He sighed and scratched his chin as he viewed the menorah from the right and then from the left. "But it isn't my father's menorah. Maybe it's all a mistake. Maybe we should stop." The sadness was beginning to appear again in his voice and in his eyes.

"No!" called Joshua. "No! It's a great menorah! Let's try some more! Please?" If they stopped, wouldn't his uncle become like Feller again? And if he became like Feller, wouldn't he die?

"Ah, Joshua. I'm tired."

"I'll do everything! You just tell me! Okay? Okay?" Joshua was surprised at how loud he was shouting. His mother wouldn't call him "the quiet one" now.

"All right. All right. We'll try a little more. Let me think. Maybe—maybe there were more decorations on it. I think there were. We'll have to make some curling vines of copper here and here . . . and here."

Hanukkah was drawing closer—four days away, then three, then two—and still Great-Uncle Otto said it wasn't his father's menorah. And with each day, his eyes grew sadder and his body seemed to sag more. Yet at the end of each afternoon, Joshua begged Great-Uncle Otto to try just one more day, one more day. And each afternoon, Otto sighed and said, "Well, well . . . I don't know . . . It's no use."

"Please!"

"All right. All right. One more day."

Finally, on the last day before Hanukkah, Otto simply sat and stared out the window, shaking his head again and again.

"Uncle Otto," Joshua called. "Please. Please. Look at what I'm doing. I'm making this tube curve some more. Maybe we still didn't curve the tubes enough." Joshua twisted and turned the copper stems desperately, hoping each new bend would be the right one, the one that would make his great-uncle's face shine like the menorah. Otto just shook his head.

"No. No. It's hopeless," said Great-Uncle Otto. "This isn't my father's menorah. It's hopeless, Joshua, hopeless. Put it on the shelf in the back room. Let it rest. Tomorrow is Hanukkah, and there are no more days, and I'm too tired to work on it anymore. Some other year, some other Hanukkah, maybe we'll try again." Uncle Otto sighed and slumped back in his chair.

Joshua was close to crying. "But . . . but . . . it's beautiful! It's beautiful, no matter what! And we worked so hard! And it was so much fun. And you were so happy making it."

"I know, Joshua, I know. I wanted to make the menorah come to life again. To give your parents a remembrance of the past. And I can't. Let it sleep on the shelf. Next year maybe. We'll see."

Joshua walked home slowly, downcast and silent. Great-Uncle Otto had looked so old. He seemed to move in slow motion, like Feller had at the end.

That night, the next morning, and all afternoon, the house bustled with his mother's preparations for Hanukkah. And though Joshua helped with the final cleaning, his thoughts were with Great-Uncle Otto sitting in a corner of the living room, staring at something far beyond the walls. Several times Joshua asked if he could get his uncle anything—the newspapers, soda, tea—but each time, his uncle shook his head slowly to say no while his hands trembled more than ever. If only there was something he could do. If only, somehow, he could make that menorah become Uncle Otto's father's father's menorah.

Toward evening, Joshua suddenly had an idea. It might work, he thought. It might. But there was hardly any time left. He grabbed his coat and raced out the door to the corner, then ran down the avenue the four long blocks to the repair shop.

At the shop, Joshua jiggled the key the way his great-uncle had shown him, and the big iron door swung open. Quickly he went toward the back of the shop, to the shelf holding the menorah. There it stood in the dim light, a shining crown waiting to be worn.

Joshua stood on a chair, took the menorah from the shelf, and put it carefully on the table. He studied it for a moment, scarcely breathing. Could he do it? Some part of him was fighting desperately against it, against this crazy idea. He'd never done anything like this before, in all his life.

No more thinking! No more! Joshua suddenly pushed the menorah off the worktable. It fell to the floor with a great metallic crash. He felt a streak of pain in his throat. The arms of the menorah were all bent sideways, out of shape. For a second, Joshua felt as if he were the very boy his great-uncle had been so many years ago, standing in dread before the wrecked menorah.

He paused for a moment. hardy breathing. It had to work! Then he started to bend each thin copper tube back into place. He put the menorah on the table from time to time, to examine it the way Great-Uncle Otto had, with one eye closed.

"Not yet," he murmured. "Not yet."

Joshua readjusted two of the arms, then stepped back to study the result, again. Better. Better. He took a sheet of rough sandpaper from the workbench at the front of the shop and rubbed it across the arms of the menorah, then across the wooden base.

Yes. That was good. Now it was an old, bent menorah instead of a brand new one. Now it was a 200-year-old menorah that had been dropped and fixed, and had been used again and again. If only he could work some more.

But it was late. His aunts and uncles and cousins must be arriving by now. His mother and father would be furious with him for not being there.

He slipped the menorah into a brown bag, then hurried out of the shop, jiggling the key to lock the door. With the bag in his hand, Joshua started to half-run, half-walk toward home. He felt a growing tightness in his chest, as he did when he had to stand up in front of the class and give a report. What would Great Uncle Otto think? Would it just make him sadder? Had he ruined everything?

As Joshua reached his front door, he could hear voices and laughter overflowing from the living room. His parents would be doubly furious. But it would be worth it if only this helped Uncle Otto.

With his coat still on, Joshua walked past the kitchen and paused. The living room was filled with all his relatives. In a distant corner, he could see Great-Uncle Otto sitting in the same place he'd been all day, alone among the bustle of people. Lost, just like Feller.

"Joshua! Where have you been! You're late!" his mother called. "Take off your coat and hurry. We've all been waiting. It's time to light the candles."

Joshua held up the brown paper bag. "But there's . . . there's a present."

"We'll have time for presents later," said his father.

"But it's from Uncle Otto," said Joshua, pulling the menorah from the bag. "It's for you and Mom. Uncle Otto made it for you, just like his old menorah from Europe." He turned toward his great-uncle. "Does it look okay, Uncle Otto? I . . . I tried to fix it so it would be like when you dropped it, and your father straightened it, and all."

He studied his great-uncle anxiously to see if he was looking. But Great-Uncle Otto was staring at Joshua's face rather than at the menorah.

"It's absolutely beautiful," said Joshua's mother.

"It's a real old-fashioned menorah," his aunt added.

"Like an antique," someone else said.

Great-Uncle Otto nodded again and again as his hair floated upward. "Now I see . . . now I see what was missing," he said softly.

"So many people, so much love. All the love our menorah had seen over the years. That's what was missing. The love. You've added it, Joshua, for me. We can make things with our hands, yes, but a real menorah we can only make with our hearts. Now this is a real menorah, the menorah that can never be broken. Thank you, Joshua, for bringing it back to life."

It wasn't all clear to him, but Joshua felt like leaping into the air. It had worked! Somehow, it had worked!

His father took the menorah and set it down gently on the table. "Otto," he said, "this menorah is a mitzvah, an act of goodness for all of us. Thank you for making this beautiful thing."

"I didn't make it. Joshua did. It's his mitzvah, not mine," said Great-Uncle Otto, his voice gathering strength. "But listen, a menorah isn't a menorah until its candles are lit. The menorah is begging for lights!"

Though it was a solemn moment, Joshua couldn't help smiling as he placed the candles in the menorah, for this was the great-uncle of the repair shop, the uncle of the booming voice and grandly waving arm.

Joshua took his great-uncle's hand, and helped him to light the center candle of the menorah. Then he carefully gave the *shammash* to his father to light the first candle on the far right. As the blessings were said, the candle flames flickered with every breath.

There was laughter in the room now, and voices, as Great-Uncle Otto began to sing the old Hanukkah song "Maoz Tsur." All the uncles and aunts joined in, and then the children began singing, too.

Great-Uncle Otto struggled up from his chair, and in the center of the room, crippled and stiff, slowly started to dance. Joshua took one trembling hand while his father took the other, to form a circle with him. And while all three turned slowly to the singing, the flames of the menorah, the old menorah of Europe, nodded and shook and danced with them.

Joshua knew he would remember the happiness in his uncle's face forever. Yes, this would be his own special memory, his own story, the one he would tell his children someday: the Hanukkah of his Great-Uncle Otto, whose hair floated as he danced, as if he were light as a bird.

Three

Test Your Holiday Smarts

Hanukkah Brain Teasers

What Day of Hanukkah Is It?

1. What day is two days before three days after the second day of Hanukkah?

2. What day is one day before four days after three days before the eighth day of Hanukkah?

3. What day is one day before two days after one day before two days after the fifth day of Hanukkah?

The Cohens

The Cohens have three daughters. Each daughter has one brother. How many children do the Cohens have?

Four Pennies and Three Cups

Four pennies were given to you as Hanukkah gelt, and three cups. How would you put the  pennies in the cups so there is an odd number of pennies in each cup?

Hanukkah Gelt

Michael was given two bills totaling $25. If one of those bills is not a $5 bill, what bills was he given?

More Hanukkah Gelt

Nathan's grandfather offered to give either Nathan $10 in Hanukkah gelt or start with 10 cents the first night and double the gelt he would give each night until the eighth night of Hanukkah. Which option should Nathan choose?

(Answers on pages 186–187)

Hanukkah Fun

Even More Hanukkah Gelt

Shoshana counted her Hanukkah gelt. She had five bills totaling $61. None were $20 bills. None were $10 bills. What bills did she have?

A Boatload of Mystery

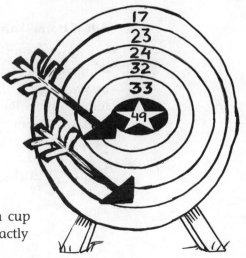

There was a Hanukkah party on an island. The guests got there in small motor boats, the only boats permitted on the lake that surrounds the island. When they reached the island, their host picked them up in a van. The van was too big to fit in a motor boat. If the van couldn't be converted into a boat and the van was not dropped on the island from above, how did the van get on the island?

Hanukkah Hugs

If each person at the Hanukkah party hugged each other person and there were six hugs, how many people were there at the party?

Family Fun

A baker's brother came home for Hanukkah, but the baker's brother who came home for Hanukkah has no brother. Please explain.

44 – 1 = 45?

How can you get 45 by subtracting one from 44?

Bull's-eye

Sharon was given a target and a set of suction cup darts as a Hanukkah gift. How can she score exactly 100?

A Sign of Confusion

Jeremy and Josh were going from one town to the next on their way to a Hanukkah party. They came to a crossroads and the sign with directions printed on it was on the ground. Jeremy feared they would get lost, but Josh knew what to do. He simply stuck the sign in the ground, looked at it for a moment, and said, "Let's go." They did and soon were at the party. How did Josh know how to set the sign?

The Man in Black

Morris is on his way to a Hanukkah party. He's dressed in black—black shirt, black pants, black hat, black socks, black shoes. All the streetlights are off. He crosses the street just as a car with its headlights turned off rounds the corner. Morris doesn't see the car, but the driver sees Morris. How can this be?

Edith's Sons

Edith went to a Hanukkah party with her two sons. The two sons were born on the same day of the same year but they were not twins. How is this possible?

A Hot Hanukkah

Zoe celebrates Hanukkah for eight days every summer, beginning on the twenty-fifth of Kislev. But if Kislev is the Hebrew month beginning in November or December, why does Zoe celebrate Hanukkah in the summer?

Spencer's Hanukkah Candles

Spencer has some Hanukkah candles. All but three of them are white. All but three of them are blue. All but three of them are green. All but three of them are yellow. How many Hanukkah candles does Spencer have?

What's Wrong Here?

It was the first night of Hanukkah. The moon was full as Eddie lit the *shammash*, and then with the *shammash* he lit the one yellow candle in his menorah. What's wrong here?

One Candle Is Carrying Holiday Weight

You have eight candles. Each candle weighs exactly the same as each of the others, except one, which weighs just a little more. If you used a balance scale, and you used it just twice, how would you find the heavier candle?

Bright Brain Teasers

Jacob, Jacob, Candle Maker

Jacob makes Hanukkah candles out of rectangular sticks of wax. He wraps the wax around a wick, shapes and shaves the wax into a candle. From each stick of wax he scrapes off one-third of the wax to make one candle. He saves the scraped-off wax and uses it to make more candles. With just 30 sticks of wax, can Jacob make all 44 candles he will need for Hanukkah?

(Answers on pages 187–189)

Tricky Wick

If the wick Deborah bought for her Hanukkah oil lights was three feet plus half its length long, how long was the wick?

Two Candles

One candle will burn for 50 minutes. Another candle will burn for 40 minutes. If both are lit at the same moment, when will one have twice as much burning time left as the other?

Three Candles

Three candles, each a half inch wide, are set three inches apart. How far apart is the first candle from the third?

Which Do You Light First?

It's the last day of Hanukkah. You have a match, eight candles in your menorah, and a *shammash*. Which do you light first?

Oops!

What would happen if you were to strike a match to light a Hanukkah candle in a sealed room filled with methane gas?

Selling His Way to Success?

Explain how a businessman became a millionaire by buying boxes of candles for $5 each and selling them for $4 each.

A Windy Night

It's the fourth night of Hanukkah. Your electric menorah is lit. It's by an open southern window and there is a 24-mile-per-hour northerly wind. How many Hanukkah lights will the wind extinguish?

Hanukkah Hunger

Ilana, Sarah, Aaron, Jennifer, and Donnie ate *sufganiyot*. Ilana ate more than Donnie and less than Aaron. Aaron ate less than Sarah and more than Ilana. Who ate the most?

The Clever Hostess

Nine children came to visit. Unfortunately, there were only eight *sufganiyot*. The hostess said, "That's not a problem." She told Becky, the first child, to wait. Then she gave the second child the first *sufganiyah*, the third child the second *sufganiyah*, the fourth child the third *sufganiyah*, and so on. She gave the eighth child the seventh *sufganiyah*. Then she gave Becky the one remaining *sufganiyah*. Did this clever hostess satisfy all her guests?

Tasty Brain Teasers

Latke, Latke

If it takes five minutes to fry one latke, how many minutes would it take to fry two latkes?

Latkes on Schedule

If you have five latkes and eat one every half an hour, how long will the five latkes last?

Fathers and Sons

Two fathers and two sons are eating latkes. If each eats one latke, how is it possible that, altogether, they eat just three latkes?

The Large Latke

What is the weight of a latke that weighs two pounds plus half its weight?

(Answers on pages 189–190)

Measure Out the Oil

If you have a three-cup jar and a five-cup jar, how would you measure out exactly four cups of oil?

Test Your Hanukkah Thinking Skills

1. If there are three latkes and you take away two, how many do you have?

2. Mendel fills his *sufganiyot* with lots of jelly. Rachel puts just a little jelly in each of her *sufganiyot*. Which would weigh more, a pound of Mendel's *sufganiyot* or a pound of Rachel's?

3. An Englishman played dreidel with his widow's sister. If there were seven pennies in the pot and his dreidel landed on *hey*, what should he do?

4. How would you play dreidel on Saturn?

5. Which would burn longer, a short, thick candle or a long, thin candle?

6. Sarah's Hanukkah party is in a one-floor house and everything is blue and white, the colors of the Israeli flag. The carpet is blue. The walls are white. The table is blue. The chairs are white. What color are the stairs?

7. You are running in a race during Hanukkah. What place are you in when you pass the runner in last place? What place are you in when you pass the second-place runner?

8. If you follow the rules for lighting the menorah each night—light one the first night, two the second night, etc.—how many candles do you use, total, during the eight nights of Hanukkah?

(Answers on page 190)

Directions: *Match the items from the left column with those in the right column. There is one match per item.*

Twenty Questions

1. Hebrew month when Hanukkah begins
2. Number of letters on a dreidel
3. Source of oil used in the Temple
4. Latkes are made from ___
5. Number of days in Hanukkah
6. Who witnessed the murder of her own seven sons?
7. Who recaptured the Temple?
8. Besides latkes, what special food do we eat on Hanukkah?
9. The word Hanukkah means ___
10. Where does the story of Hanukkah begin?
11. What light always burned in the Temple?
12. What were the Jews forced to do?
13. Who said, "Whoever is for the Lord our God follow me!"?
14. On the first night of Hanukkah, we say ___ blessings.
15. In Israel, the dreidel has what different letter on it?
16. The Hebrew word for "dreidel" is ___
17. How many candles are in a Hanukkah candle box?
18. "Gelt" is another word for ___
19. Who did Judith defeat?
20. Who is the king who led the battle against the Jews?

(Answers on page 191)

A. Four
B. Hannah
C. Antiochus IV
D. *Sufganiyot*
E. Bow to idols
F. Maccabees
G. Holofernes
H. Kislev
I. *Ner Tamid*
J. Money
K. Potatoes
L. Three
M. 44
N. The letter *peh*
O. Olives
P. Eight
Q. Dedication
R. *Sivivon*
S. Mattathias
T. Judea

Mendel's Crazy Hanukkah Quiz

1. This woman:
A. had a light dinner.
B. ate a candle and lit a latke.
C. has a light case of heartburn.

3. This menorah:
A. is for people who <u>really</u> love Hanukkah.
B. is for people with extra candles.

2. This jelly doughnut:
A. works in a bakery.
B. is studying to be a babke.
C. has dreidels in his brief case.

4. This cow:
A. is filled with jelly.
B. just lit her <u>moon</u>orah.
C. likes to tell elephant jokes.

(Answers on page 191)

Mendel's Crazy Hanukkah Quiz

5. This dreidel:
A. doesn't want to play.
B. is pointless.
C. is dizzy and pointless.

7. This man:
A. is light headed.
B. is one candle short
   of a menorah.
C. is a drip.
D. is Mendel.

6. This candle:
A. just got her wick done.
B. is going out tonight.

Hanukkah Mazes

Find a Path Through the Menorah

Start

End

(Answers on page 192)

Help This Boy
Light His Menorah

(Answers on page 193)

Find a Path
to the Menorah

Start

(Answers on page 194)

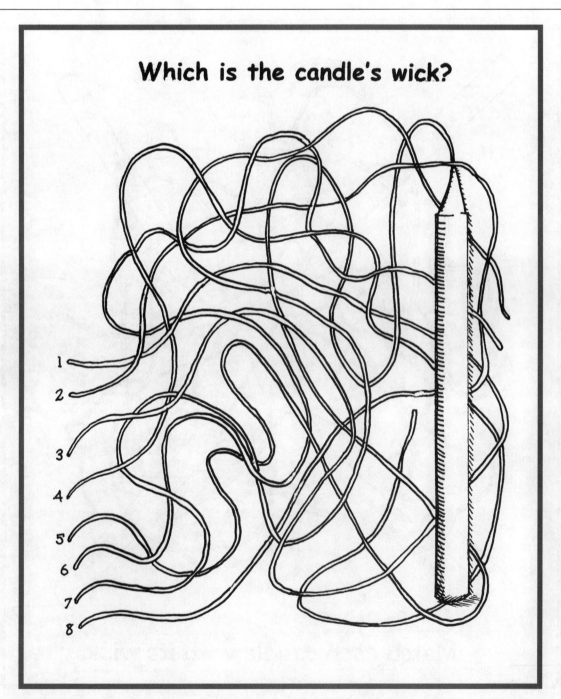

Which is the candle's wick?

(Answers on page 194)

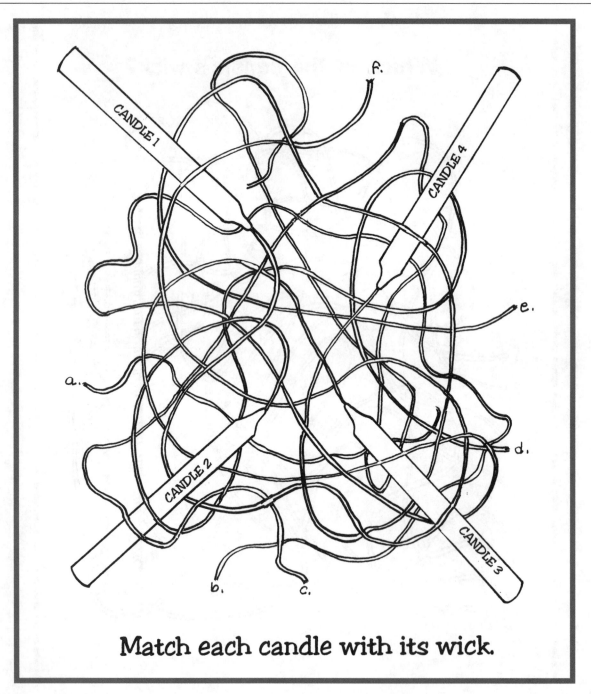

Match each candle with its wick.

(Answers on page 195)

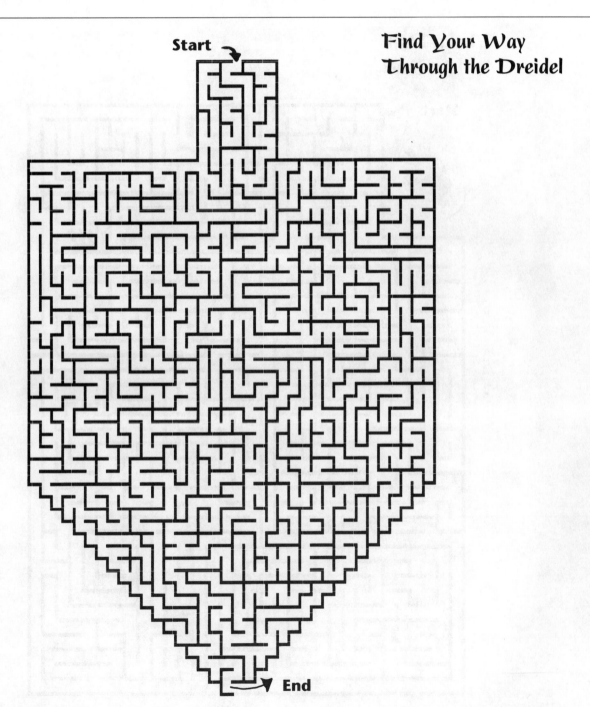

Start

End

Find Your Way
Through the Dreidel

(Answers on page 195)

Find a Path to the Gimel

Start

(Answers on page 196)

Find a Path to the Oil

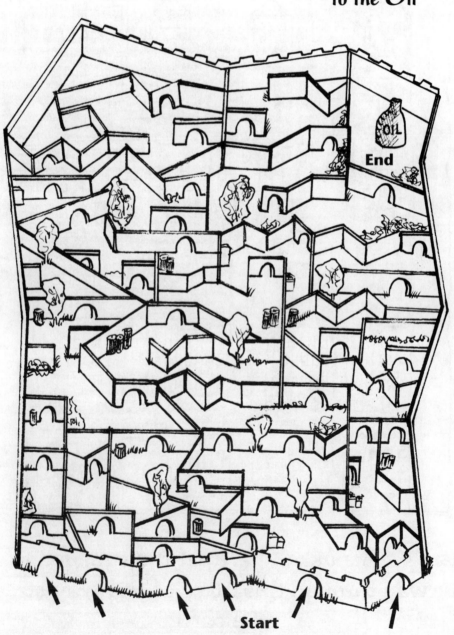

(Answers on page 197)

Start

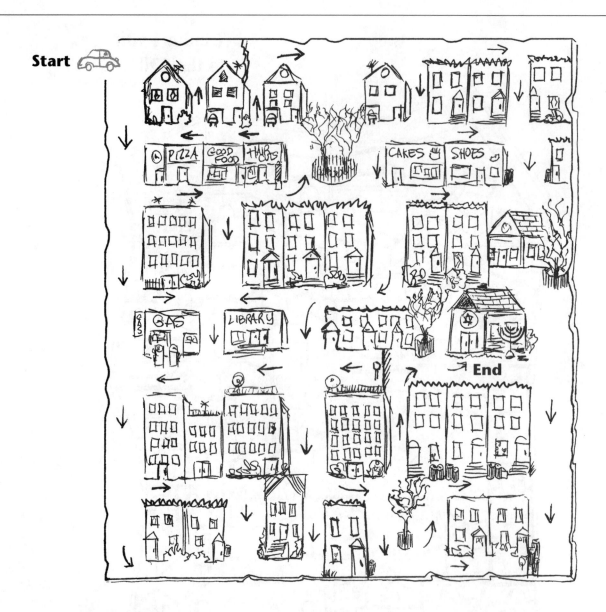

There's a Hanukkah party at the synagogue. Find your way through this maze of one-way streets to the party.

(Answers on page 198)

Games

The word *sivivon* means "to turn around" in Hebrew. How appropriate for a dreidel! The four letters printed on the sides of every dreidel (*nun, gimel, hey, shin*) stand for the Hebrew declaration *Nes gadol haya sham*—"A great miracle happened there." This, of course, refers to the miracle of finding that little bit of oil to light the menorah for eight whole days. If you were playing the dreidel game in Israel, the fourth letter would be a *pey* instead of a *shin*, changing the saying to "A great miracle happened here." And they do play dreidel in Israel. In fact, the dreidel game is played all over the world during Hanukkah, and every game is different. Even so, the basics are the same:

I Have a Little Dreidel … And a Lot of Fun!

- Any number of people can play.

- Each player begins the game with an equal number of game pieces—about 10 to 15—which can be pennies (or larger coins for big spenders), raisins, nuts, chocolate chips, gelt, M&Ms, or any number of things.

- Start the game with each person putting one game piece (we'll use raisins as an example) into the center of the circle (the "pot"). Everyone should help refill the pot when it becomes empty.

- Spin the dreidel once when it's your turn, after which the real fun begins.

- If you land on *nun* נ, that means *nisht*—nothing. Sit back and relax, because you do nothing on this turn!

- If you land on *gimel* ג, in the game that means *gantz* (everything). You get everything in the pot! Mazel tov!

- The letter *hey* ה in the game means *halb*, or "half." If you land on *hey*, you get half of the raisins in the pot. (You can be greedy for odd numbers. For example, if there are nine raisins in the pot, take five.)

- Last and certainly least is *shin* ש, which means *shtel* (put in). You have to add a raisin to the pot.

When you run out of raisins, you've lost the game! (Unless someone is willing to loan you a raisin or two.)

When one player lands on *gimel*, the round is over. You could time the game instead: After a certain amount of time, the player with the most raisins wins that round.

For a fun way to share a Hanukkah gift with others, play the dreidel game for *tzedakah*, charity. Donate the pot to charity, perhaps with a matching contribution from your parents, and make the holidays happy for everyone.

Round and Round It Goes, Where It Lands, Nobody Knows!

Will I get a gimel?
Is the shin *a shoe-in?*
Bet a nickel on nun.
I'm hoping for hey!

Is the traditional dreidel game not rich enough for your blood? Then try this riskier version, best for four players (but fun for any group of two or more).

First, you'll need a game grid. Make it four columns across—one for each letter on the dreidel—and as many rows as you'd like going down (each row signifies a spin of the dreidel). You'll also need game pieces to play for, which can be any number of things: coins, candies, or poker chips, to name a few. Now you're ready to play!

Each player chooses a different letter of the dreidel (which is why this game is best for four competitors, but you'll see that it can be played by any number of people, as long as they are willing to place a bet). Start by having each player bet one game piece.

Take turns spinning the dreidel, and after it lands each time use the game grid to record which letter it landed on, and then spin again—and again and again. If a player feels confident after winning a spin or two, he or she can risk more by adding one or more game pieces to the pot, which has to be matched by each player who doesn't want to "fold" at that point.

When all the spinning has made you dizzy, tally up how many times each

letter was landed upon. If you chose that letter, you win Round 1—and the pot!

Feel free to add to or change the rules. For example, you may want everyone to pick new letters after every spin. Or players can switch letters after a round or two to try their luck at, say, *gimel* instead of *shin*, but you should all decide if that decision will cost the player a game piece or two. Make sure that the rules apply to everyone and that you record all the necessary information.

Dreidel of Fortune

Play "Wheel of Fortune" Hanukkah style. The game begins with a "bank" of pieces of whatever gelt you are using. One person will play the part of Master of Ceremonies. The other participants (you'll need at least two more) will take turns spinning the dreidel. If the dreidel lands on *hey* or *shin*, that player gets a chance to guess a letter in one of the puzzles. If you land on *gimel*, you can make two guesses. If you spin a *nun* you get no chance to guess and you lose your turn. For each letter you guess correctly, you add (from the bank) two pieces of whatever gelt you are playing for to your pot. If there are two of the letter you guessed, you add four pieces of gelt (2 x 2) to your pot, and so on. However, if you decide to buy a vowel, you must pay (back to the bank) two pieces of gelt. If you solve the puzzle, you keep your pot. The pots of all other players are returned to the bank.

If you win, take another spin and you will then:

- 🪙 Lose a turn if you land on the letter *nun*.

- 🪙 Win four pieces from the bank of whatever gelt you are playing with if you land on *gimel*.

- 🪙 Win three pieces of gelt if you land on *hey*.

- 🪙 Win two pieces of gelt if you land on *shin*.

You are provided with eight "Dreidel of Fortune" puzzles as examples, or the Master of Ceremonies may want to write his or her own. On the next page you'll find eight "Dreidel of Fortune" puzzle blanks you can use. The letters for these blanks are on page 199.

(Answers on page 199)

Puzzle #1: People

_____

Puzzle #2: Thing

_____

Puzzle #3: Phrase

_____

Puzzle #4: Thing

_____

Puzzle #5: Person

_____

Puzzle #6: Before and After

_____

Puzzle #7: Things

_____

Puzzle #8: Event

_____

This is a game to test your Hanukkah knowledge if you play alone. If you play with others, you can test yourself *and* earn gelt!

Begin with a pot of pennies, raisins, or other gelt. There are two statements for each number, but only one is correct. On the dreidel next to the correct statement, draw a *gimel* ﬡ. Draw a *nun* ﬡ on the dreidel next to the incorrect statement. (Make photocopies of this page before you mark it up so that everyone can play by marking the dreidels.)

When you and your friends have completed the test, consult the answers and note how many you got correct.

Then, take turns spinning the dreidel. Take 3 pennies for a *gimel*, 2 for a *hey*, 1 for a *nun*, and none for a *shin*. But here's the catch: In this game of dreidel, you are allowed only as many spins as the number of correct answers you have. When you have spun for each of your correct answers, you are out of the game. How much you earn before that point is up to chance.

The last person to spin is a Hanukkah genius, and he or she wins whatever is left in the pot.

Obviously, it is best to play with many people to ensure lively competition and many spins, and it is best to study up beforehand. Answer all eight questions correctly and you can win it all, but answer zero correctly and you're broke. By the end of the game, your head might be spinning along with the dreidel!

A Testy Game of Dreidel

1. a. Judith, a Hanukkah heroine, had seven sons.

    b. Hannah, a Hanukkah heroine, had seven sons.

2. a. Hanukkah begins on the twenty-fifth of the Hebrew month of Kislev.

   b. Hanukkah begins on the twenty-fifth of the Hebrew month of Tevet.

3. a. Judah Maccabee had five brothers.

    b. Judah Maccabee had four brothers.

(Answers on page 199)

4. a. Rosh Hodesh, which celebrates a new month, sometimes occurs during Hanukkah.

 b. Rosh Hodesh, which celebrates a new month, always occurs during Hanukkah.

5. a. The full name of the Syrian king that the Maccabees defeated was Antiochus IV.

 b. The full name of the Syrian king that the Maccabees defeated was Antiochus VI.

6. a. There are 44 candles in a box of Hanukkah candles.

 b. There are 35 candles in a box of Hanukkah candles.

7. a. In Israel, the four letters on the dreidel are *nun, gimel, hey, shin.*

 b. In Israel, the four letters on the dreidel are *nun, gimel, hey, pey.*

8. a. Hanukkah is the only Jewish holiday to last eight days.

b. Hanukkah is not the only Jewish holiday to last eight days.

Flip 'n Fry

This game lets you test your latke-flipping skills.

Here's how you play: After making your latke and frying pan, try to flip the latke onto the pan. Make sure you practice on your own, and then challenge a friend to a flipping contest. Whoever flips the latke into the pan the most times in a row gets a latke meal—cooked by the loser! (Or you can play for other treats and prizes. If this isn't challenging enough for you, try playing blindfolded.)

What you need:

2 jumbo craft sticks   string (12"–16" long)
tape   scissors
paper plate   piece of cardboard
aluminum foil   colored markers
hole punch   (if desired)

What to do:

1. Take two craft sticks and tape them together to make a longer stick–this will be your frying pan handle.

2. Attach the craft sticks to the paper plate with tape or glue to make a frying pan.

3. Color, decorate, or cover the frying pan (paper plate) in aluminum foil.

5. Take the hole punch and punch a hole in the top of the paper plate, on the side opposite the handle, and tie one end of the string to it.

6. To make your latke, just cut a circle out of a piece of cardboard, making sure it is smaller than your frying pan.

7. Punch a hole near the edge of the "latke" and tie the other end of the piece of string through this hole, connecting the latke to the pan. Now you're ready to flip 'n fry!

Candle Cunning

If you have a few minutes before your family lights the candles, grab a brother or sister, cousin, parent, or friend and play this fun, quick game. If you'd like, you can decide who gets to light the candles that night or say the blessing by giving that honor to the winner.

Place the entire contents of a box of Hanukkah candles between two players. Each player, in turn, gets to take one, two, three, or four candles. Each player *must* take at least one candle (but no more than four) on each turn. The player to take the last candle loses.

Magic

Hanukkah Magic

Look at these 3 candles, a red, a green, and a white.

I turn around and hold the candles behind my back.

Pick 1 candle. Hold it up. Let everyone but me see it.

Return it to my hand, the one behind my back.

The candle you picked was green.

THE TRICK: After you gave me back the candle and before I put it with the others, I scratched it. I had some of the wax under my fingernail. I looked at the color of the wax and I knew the color of the candle.

Hanukkah Gelt Magic

Look at my Hanukkah gelt.

Count the coins.

Now, I'll spill the coins
into your hand.

Count the coins
again.

Hey, that's
more.

The trick: Before your begin, open the book to the middle.   Put a few
coins on the open page.   Then hide a few on inside pages.   When you
spill the coins into your friend's hand, the coins he saw *and* the
hidden coins will spill out.

Broken Candle Magic

The Trick: Hidden in the bag was an unbroken candle, the same color as the one you broke. Inside the bag, too, is some tape folded so it's sticky on both sides. One sticky side is taped to the inside of the bag and the other side is not. When you put the broken candle in the bag you were careful to stick it to the tape. When you turned the bag upside down only the unbroken candle fell out.

More Candle Magic

Here are 5 Hanukkah candles.
Each is a different color.

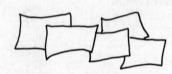

You say, "I'll write a
color on a each slip
of paper." Do that.

Say, "I crumple each of the
papers." Do that. Then throw
the papers into a hat.

You take a paper from
the hat and choose a
candle, seemingly
at random.

Show everyone the paper.

"Look!" you say. "That's
the color of the candle."

The trick: You wrote "blue" on each slip of paper. You crumpled
the papers and threw them into the hat before anyone had a chance
to look at them. Of course, after you amaze your friends, you get rid
of the papers. Don't let anyone see you wrote "blue" on each paper.

Puzzle Fun

Hanukkah Number Phrases

What do these Hanukkah number phrases mean?
Example: 7 D in a W = Seven days in a week

1) 8 N of H

2) 44 C in a B

3) H and H 7 S

4) 4 S on a D

5) 9 C L on the 8th N of H I the S

6) A M H 9 C

7) M and H 5 S

8) H B on the 25th of K

Calculator Fun

With your calculator solve the math problem at the end of each sentence. Then turn your calculator upside down. The digits in the answer will look like letters and spell a word.

1. Before you light the Hanukkah candles you _____ 27689 X 2 =

2. When you are invited to a Hanukkah party you _____ 72 - 12 X .01 =

3. When you read a Hanukkah bummer you _____ 200 X 38 X 50 - 81 =

4. You meet your cousin at a Hanukkah party and say _____ 27 - 26.2266 =

5. To make latkes you need potatoes, onions, oil, and _____ 222 X 3 X 9 - 1 =

(Answers on pages 199–200)

Happy
Hanukkah
Re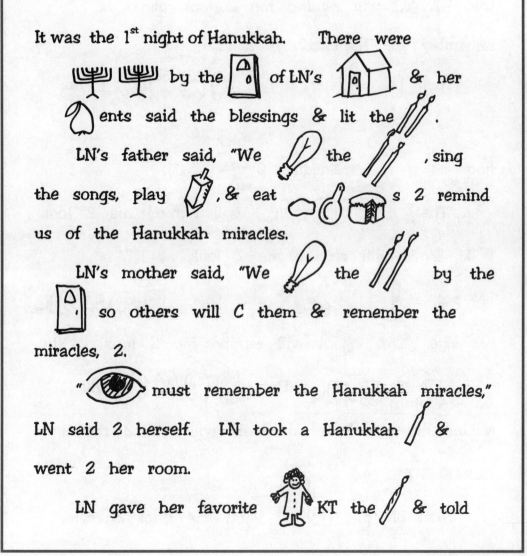

It was the 1st night of Hanukkah.   There were

[menorahs] by the [door] of LN's [house] & her

[tulip]ents said the blessings & lit the [candles].

LN's father said, "We [light] the [candles], sing

the songs, play [dreidel], & eat [latke]s 2 remind

us of the Hanukkah miracles.

LN's mother said, "We [light] the [candles] by the

[window] so others will C them & remember the

miracles, 2.

" [eye] must remember the Hanukkah miracles,"

LN said 2 herself.   LN took a Hanukkah [candle] &

went 2 her room.

LN gave her favorite [doll] KT the [candle] & told

(Continued on next page)

her about Hanukkah. LN told KT, "If  C U

holding the   will remember the Hanukkah

miracles."

Then LN put her teddy bear JJ near KT. LN

told KT, "JJ will remind me 2 look at U &

remember the Hanukkah miracles."

Then LN set her toy  on

the

pick

floor as if it were riding 2 JJ.

"The  will remind me 2 look

@ JJ & JJ will remind me 2 look at KT."

LN put a   side the .

& said, "The  will remind me 2 look @ the

. The  will

remind me 2 look @ JJ & JJ will remind me 2

look @ KT."

Then LN put  on the floor & said,

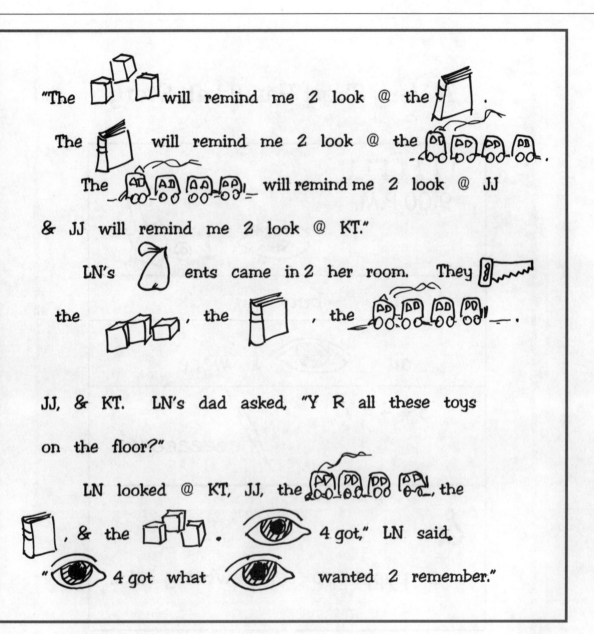

"The 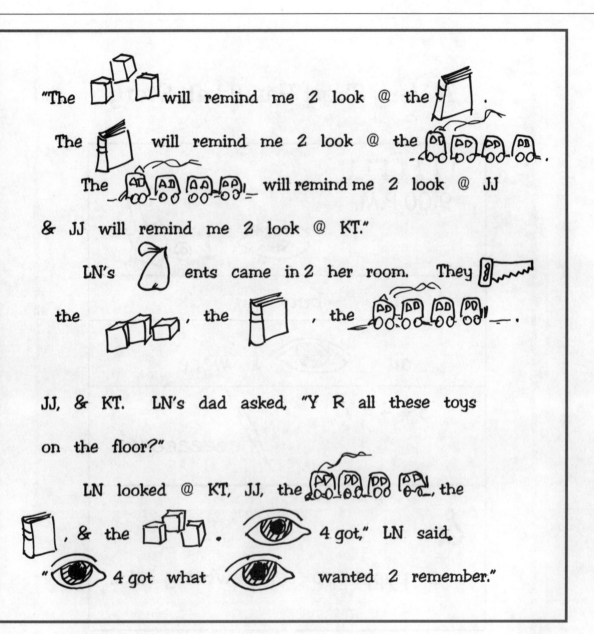 will remind me 2 look @ the 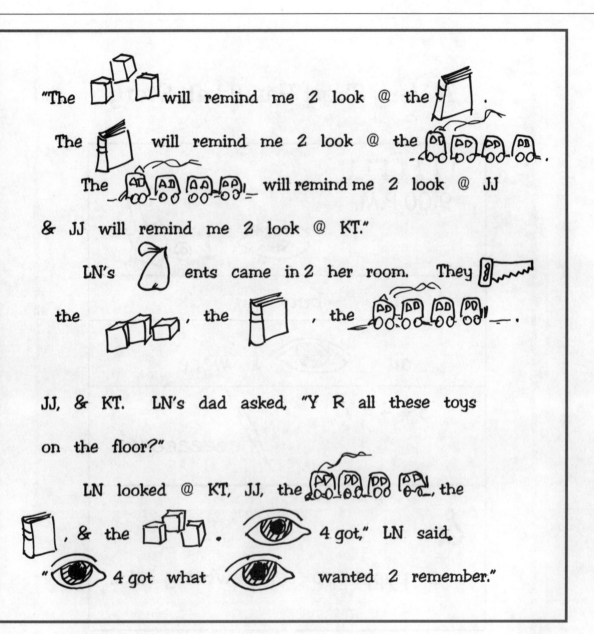.

The will remind me 2 look @ the .

The will remind me 2 look @ JJ

& JJ will remind me 2 look @ KT."

LN's ents came in 2 her room. They

the , the , the .

JJ, & KT. LN's dad asked, "Y R all these toys

on the floor?"

LN looked @ KT, JJ, the , the

, & the . 4 got," LN said.

" 4 got what wanted 2 remember."

A Very Short Hanukkah Story

<u>1 1 1 1 1 1 1</u>
9:00 P.M.

 **1 @**

but

all **1** were

3 + 4 = 7

eeeeeeeee

&

a ppppppp of strawberry cake.

(Answers on page 201)

PICTURE PUZZLES

Do you know what these are?

1- **A** 100%

2-

3-

4-

HANUKKAH
NIGHT-NIGHT

What night of Hanukkah is it when you see this sign?

(Answers on page 201)

What's written or pictured in each box? #1

1. can   dle
   ca   ndle
    c   an dle
	2. [square with small o inside]

3. <u>Hanukkah</u> 222222day	4. U R <u>2 light</u> 6:15 P.M.
5. [can drawing] dddd & PEPPER, MD	6. @ [dreidel] U win 4 + 4 = 8 ......U lose 6 + 6 = 12
7. [wavy line]	8. [fan drawing] C [menorah drawing]

(Answers on page 202)

What's written or pictured in each box? #2

1. The NME was B10	2. *Latke Latke* my plate
3. *We light 4* *day day day day* *day day day day*	4. gave Greek Armies
5. *There R* *side side* *side side* *2 a dreidel*	6. *Mattathias* *& his* 🔥🔥🔥🔥🔥

7.

H
A
R
O
N
E
M
the
T
H
G
I
L

(Answers on page 202)

What's written or pictured in each box? #3

I have dreidel	*Joke* *U*
wincandlesdow	priest
D O I O I M N M N	oil BURNED BURNED

(Answers on pages 202–203)

The Hanukkah Party

Take a look at the boxes below. Each contains a rebus-like puzzle that describes something being served at a Hanukkah party. Do you know what's being served?

1. Lat *KKKKKKKKKK*	2. N E V E S
3. Eggs y n n u s	4. ♫ -a- 🐟
5. 🥫 DDDDDDDDDD	6. LEM ade
7. G-S-E G	8. LEFT kugel

(Answers on page 203)

Peculiar Sentences

1-Look at the dialog below. What do all the two-letter words have in common?

> "Oh," Ma asked me. "Will you put the candles in the menorah, or should I? Or should Pa?"
> I said, "Ok. I'll put them in."

2- What's wrong with this sentence?

I love to to bake and eat lots and lots of sufganiyot.

3-What's peculiar about this sentence?

> I do now have great latkes recipes, likewise delicious sufganiyot.

(Answers on page 203)

THE CANDLE BOX

There are 44 candles in this box, enough for all eight
nights of Hanukkah. Can you find them all? They are written
horizontally, vertically, and diagonally. Some are written backward.

```
C A N D L E M C R C A N D L E L A T K E S R
B R H M O I G A H O U S E E L D N A C M E E
N C S E V E N N F O U R L C R S P C V Q U L
M O A B C O I D O N Y D U A X R O E B P E D
O G H N O A M L N R N O P N R T G L K F O N
E I Y R D M N E G A H J K D W N O D O P B A
L K U Y R L O D C G H U O L H J C N P N S C
D P O T G N E P L K S Q V E O H R A L I T E
N C A N D L E H I E C A N D L E M C U R W I
A M O I U I C A N D L E U C A N D L E J E K
C Y C A N D L E G C U E L D N A C K I O L P
B M E N O R A H I A S H A M A S H B N Y D U
C A N D L E B G T N P R C A N D L E H P N P
U R E L D N A C K D C A N D L E K F S Q A C
C A N D L E B U C L P T Y S E Y F O R Z C A
C A N D L E H Y A E P H F L G C A N D L E N
X K I Y T R U T N R F S D O C N C T Z K H D
C C A N D L E H D M R N T A Y O U A B V X L
A C A N D L E B L R A H N J H G F S N L K E
N G C D W R T R E C O P M E N O R A H D O W
D G B A B R F E D S L E L D N A C O N E L I
L T R O N P O U R E M B V F C A N D L E H E
E F O U R D H K C A N D L E B V C F Y T R S
C A N D L E L C A N D L E M E L D N A C O U
C A N D L E F E C A N D L E M O E L D N A C
```

(Answers on page 204)

How Many Candles?

(Answers on page 205)

How Many Dreidels?

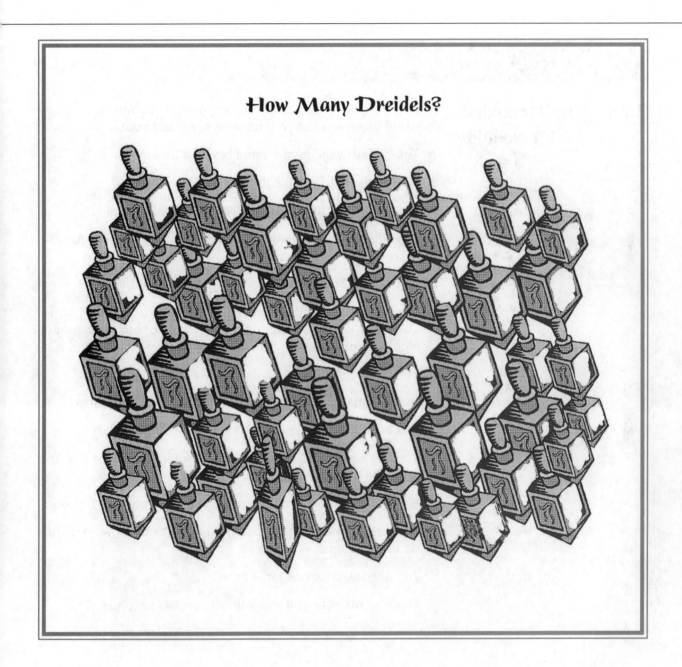

(Answers on page 205)

Hanukkah Hijinks

Test Your Hanukkah Personality

How do you eat your latkes and *sufganiyot*? Answer these questions and then see what your answers say about you!

1. You nibble at them, one small bite at a time.

2. You try to eat the whole thing in one big bite.

3. You cover the latkes with applesauce or sour cream.

4. You squeeze all the jelly out of the *sufganiyot* and eat just the jelly.

5. You like the *sufganiyot* and latkes but don't eat them.

6. First, you cut them into small pieces with a fork and knife. Then you eat each bite, one at a time, wiping your mouth with a clean napkin in between chewing.

What your latke—and *sufganiyot*—eating habits say about you.

1. You are a quiet, more reserved person.

2. You are sometimes reckless and do wild things, but you are fun to be with.

3. Nothing fazes you, but sometimes you hide your true feelings.

4. You are a risk-taker, but sometimes that can get you into sticky situations.

5. You are a strange one, aren't you?

6. You are efficient—you know how to get the job done.

Hanukkah Oddities

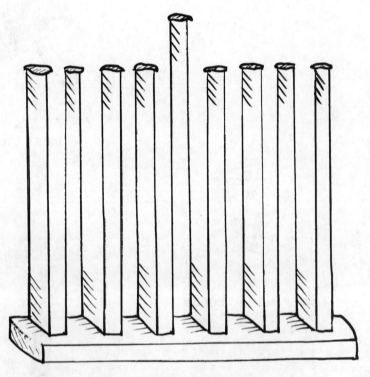

Can you tell what's odd about this menorah?

The wickless candle. There's one in every box.

An all-*nun* dreidel. For a game that never ends.

An all-*gimmel* dreidel. For children who hate To lose.

(Answers on page 205)

Unwanted Hanukkah Gifts

A mesh umbrella

A blank dreidel

Clear plastic cards

A fire-proof candle

A book,
Teach Yourself To Read

A YO
(It goes down
but doesn't come up.)

Solar-powered lantern

Lead-free pencil

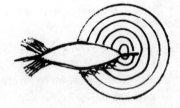

Darts and an inflatable target

Play money Hanukkah gelt

A cardboard menorah

Sugar-free sufganiyot

Fun Facts and Holiday Hints

Eight Gift Ideas for Eight Nights

1st Night: Everyone Gives/Receives from Everyone Else

In a family of eight (including parents, grandparents, and children), for example, each member is assigned a different night and must prepare a round of small gifts for everyone on that night. Of course, not everyone may be home every night of Hanukkah, but the principle is that everyone gives to everyone else or that each child exchanges gifts with all other children and the same for each parent and grandparent. In other families there could be a pre-assigned Grandparents, Parents, and Children's Nights when all the gifts come from those designated givers. Don't forget to prepare extra gifts for guests.

1ST NIGHT

2ND NIGHT

2nd Night: Homemade Gifts

Rather than "the best money can buy," try a night of homemade and handmade presents. They can be anything: a picture frame, art, jewelry, place mats, bookmarks, etc. If you cannot make your own, you might buy handmade gifts such as a personalized wooden dreidel for each person.

3rd Night: "Secret Admirer" Gifts

Before Hanukkah or on the first night prepare a bag with all the names of the participants for a later night. Ask every-

3RD NIGHT

Rules for Dreidel

Did you ever wonder where these rules for the dreidel game came from? Why is it that we take everything when we land on *gimel*? These rules come from the Yiddish words *nisht*, *gantz*, *halb*, and *shtel*. Since Hebrew and Yiddish are written using the same letters, the first letters of these words actually match the letters on the dreidel. As we know, each letter on the dreidel stands for a word in the sentence "*Nes gadol haya sham*," but it also tells us how to play the game using these Yiddish words. So the letter *nun*, for example, stands for *nes* in Hebrew and *nisht* (nothing) in Yiddish.

Escape by Dreidel: A Legend

Who invented the dreidel? According to an old legend, the Hanukkah top was dreamed up during the time of the Maccabees. When cruel Antiochus ruled Palestine, he forbade Jews to study the Torah or to gather in synagogues. To fool the king's spies, Jews would meet in small groups and study the Torah from memory. In that way, if one forgot a passage, another who remembered could teach it to him.

Teachers and pupils used to assemble secretly and study in hidden places, while one person acted as a lookout at the entrance. If soldiers were approaching, a warning was given and the group would quickly separate and hurry away through back doors and buried passages. Among the many clever tricks that were used to avoid discovery was the dreidel game. Those who were studying kept a top on the table. If a soldier managed to get by the lookout and accuse them of studying Torah, someone would grab the dreidel and spin it. As far as the soldiers could tell, the Jews had only come together to play a game.

Thus, the little Hanukkah dreidel saved the lives of many of our people.

one to pick one name but keep it secret. Then each one prepares a gift for up to a specified amount of money and wraps it nicely with the name of the recipient but not the name of the donor. On a later night of Hanukkah everyone finds a personal gift from a giver who will remain nameless. Enjoy the mystery and the surprise.

4th Night: Gelt Giving as Well as *Tzedakah* Games

Give (or ask your parents to give) everyone cash (gelt) but then make each recipient an intriguing offer: Donate a portion of your gift money to a *tzedakah* of your choice and I will match it (or maybe double or triple it). Alternatively, everyone can be asked to bring cash to be used in *tzedakah* games of dreidel or cards. The winner chooses the beneficiary of the *tzedakah*.

5th Night: Grab Bag

Ask everyone to buy one or two gifts that are less than $5 each and wrap them without names of recipients. Place them in a bag and then take turns reaching in and choosing your gift.

6TH NIGHT

6th Night: "Quality-Time" Gifts

Often after a wonderful holiday celebration we wonder why we don't spend more time together with friends and relatives. So this Hanukkah, give each other a promise of quality time together. Prepare a nice greeting card with homemade coupons or certificates that promise such things as a long-distance call, a night at the movies, a game of Monopoly, a walk on the beach, or a weekend skiing. The gift of quality time helps create family memories that are, themselves, the greatest gifts.

7TH NIGHT

7th Night: Edible Gifts and Canned Goods for the Homeless

Make it a night to bring something tasty, whether it is homemade or not (such as sugar cookies in Hanukkah shapes or chocolate gelt). But also bring canned goods that are easily transported to shelters for the hungry, or make a donation to an organization that helps feed the hungry, such as Mazon.

8TH NIGHT

8th Night: Give of Yourself

On this evening all gifts must involve a promise of some future personal service. For example, "I promise to give my mother an hour of housecleaning without complaint" or "to give my brother a home-cooked meal," or "to read my child a whole book," or "to teach my friend to play guitar."

Hanukkah Hellos

Hanukkah is a time for families to come together, but sometimes that's just impossible. Do your grandparents live in Florida? Is your older brother or sister away at school? Did your best friend just move to another state? Well, now it's time to share your Hanukkah fun with a telephone call.

Do your grandparents bake you cookies and other delicious treats? Hanukkah is the time to thank them and return the favor by sending them your own homemade cookies. Many kinds (for example, chocolate chip, sugar, and butter cookies) can be made into Hanukkah cookies. Use cookie cutters in the shape of dreidels, menorahs, and Stars of David to form your cookies, then sprinkle them with blue and white sprinkles or blue-colored sugar crystals.

Along with the cookies, send your own drawings of Hanukkah scenes—grandparents love those kinds of things. You could make a picture of the oil being discovered or of the Jews refusing to bow down to idols. Or make a beautiful menorah with paints and crayons.

Mix and match these ideas to let those close to you know you love them. And be sure to include a Hanukkah card created and signed by you!

Portable Hanukkah Party

People will love to receive a package from you that's been custom made just for them. You could send your sister at college a portable Hanukkah party so she could celebrate with her friends. Include a Hanukkah paper tablecloth, napkins, and a small, non-breakable menorah—and don't forget to include candles, dreidels, and gelt. You might also make one of the Star of David decorations in the following crafts section and include it in the package.

Tidbits of Hanukkah Wisdom

Latkes are like SUVs. The big ones need lots of oil.

Set aside a few hours for yourself each night of Hanukkah. By the end of the holiday, you'll have a whole day with nothing to do.

The sooner you fall behind on your Hanukkah shopping, the more time you'll have to catch up.

Before you light your Hanukkah candles, remember to light the *shammash*. Before you light the *shammash*, remember to light the match.

About 8.4 percent of all Hanukkah candles don't have wicks. About 14.9 percent of all Hanukkah gifts are useless. About 23 percent of all jelly-filled *sufganiyot* don't have enough jelly. And about 58.9 percent of all statistics are made up.

If you have a little dreidel and you made it out of clay, you've got a lot of time on your hands and a lot of clay under your fingernails.

Before a Hanukkah party, if everything seems to be ready, you're obviously overlooking something.

Crafts

Dough Menorah

*Flour isn't just for food,
as you'll soon know.
So go and be creative
with your dough!*

As you know, it is customary to place your menorah by the window of your house so that the beauty of its light can be shared by all who pass by. With these crafty ideas, the light won't be the only beautiful thing to see; your menorah itself will attract attention, too!

What you need:

newspaper or wax paper to protect work surface
2 cups flour
1 cup salt
1 cup water
large mixing bowl
food coloring in various colors
Hanukkah candles
cookie sheet
aluminum foil
piece of sturdy cardboard (approximately 7" x 15")

What to do:

1. Cover a flat surface with newspaper or wax paper to protect it from food coloring stains.

2. Mix the flour, salt, and water together in the large bowl to make dough.

3. Knead the dough with your hands on a flat surface until it is smooth, adding more flour if the dough is too sticky.

4. Divide the dough into 3 lumps. Add about 5–6 drops of different colored food coloring to each lump, then knead them each again to mix in the color. Good Hanukkah colors are blue, yellow, and white (no coloring), but be as original as you want! (Note: Food coloring may temporarily stain your hands so you should wash them between lumps to prevent the colors from mixing together.)

5. Take a small ball of dough from one of the lumps and put it to the side. Then form each lump into a long, snakelike roll. Braid the 3 rolls together, as you would a loaf of challah, being careful not to tear the dough.

6. Cover the cookie sheet with aluminum foil. Then place the braided dough on it.

7. After choosing a set of Hanukkah candles to last all 8 nights (44 candles total), use one to make 8 holes in your braided menorah, anywhere you like. Wiggle the candle around a bit to make sure the hole is big enough and deep enough, but don't make the hole too big—you don't want loose candles!

8. Choose a spot on the menorah for the *shammash*. Place the leftover ball of dough on that spot and gently push it down onto the braid. Then use a candle to make a hole for the *shammash*, just as you did for the other candles.

9. Bake your menorah in a 300° F. oven for 30 minutes.

10. Take the menorah out of the oven to cool and harden completely. Place the menorah on a piece of cardboard that has been painted or covered with aluminum foil.

Optional: Cover your menorah with shellac after it has hardened so the dough doesn't crack and crumble.

What you need:

self-hardening clay, about 1½ lbs.
ruler
butter knife
Hanukkah candles
sheet of sturdy cardboard, covered with aluminum foil
paintbrush
acrylic or tempera paint in assorted colors

Homemade Hanukkah Menorah

*Even though it's made out of clay
it's perfect for a bright holiday.*

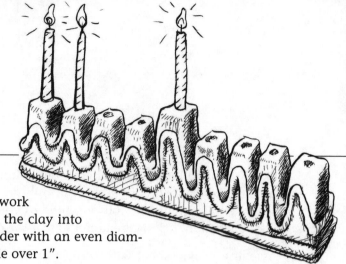

What to do:

1. On a clean work surface, roll the clay into a long cylinder with an even diameter of a little over 1".

2. Measure the cylinder and mark off 10 even lengths (about 1" each).

3. Cut eight of these lengths, and leave the last two uncut (these will be the taller *shammash*). If the cylinders flatten when cut, gently reshape them.

4. Using a Hanukkah candle, make a hole in 1 end of each cylinder, deep enough to hold a lighted candle. Again, reshape gently.

5. On the cardboard base, line up the cylinders side by side, with the one for the *shammash* in the center. Gently press the sides of the cylinders together, using water to make them stick. (Some separation may occur when the menorah dries.)

6. To decorate your menorah, roll out a thin coil of clay to twine around the bottom or sides. To help clay decorations adhere to the menorah, brush both surfaces with water before attaching.

7. Let the finished menorah dry for a day or two (it will become lighter in color as it dries), and then paint it in bright colors and allow the paint to dry.

Menorah Wall Hanging

*You can add a flame each Hanukkah night
And you won't need a match to make the candlelight.*

What you need:

marker
ruler
yellow, dark blue, and white felt
scissors
12" x 18" blue poster board (or a piece of cardboard painted blue)
white glue
Velcro
hole punch
18" piece of cord or string

What to do:

1. Make the candles: Cut nine 3" x 1" candles from white felt.

2. Make the flames: Cut 9 flame shapes from yellow felt.

3. Make the candleholders: From the dark blue felt, cut eight 2" squares and one 3" x 2" rectangle for the bottom of the candles.

4. Assemble the menorah: Take the blue poster board and place it on a flat surface. Glue the dark blue felt candleholders along the lower edge by spacing them equally apart and placing the larger candleholder in the middle or at either end for the *shammash*.

5. Attach the candles: Glue a white felt candle above each holder.

6. Attach the Velcro: Cut 9 small Velcro strips and glue 1 side above each candle. Glue the matching Velcro strip to the back of each yellow felt flame.

7. Attach the hanging cord: Punch 2 holes along the top of the poster board, close to either end. Tie the ends of the cord or string through the holes, and your menorah is ready for hanging.

8. Add a felt "flame" to your hanging menorah each night of Hanukkah—and don't forget the *shammash*!

A Handy Menorah

*Your parents will love
this menorah of HANDles!*

What you need:

newspaper or paper towels
finger paint (any dark color)
large paint brush
large piece of light-colored construction paper
scissors
piece of yellow or orange construction paper
clear tape

What to do:

1. Lay down some newspaper or paper towels on a table or an uncarpeted floor.

2. Use the paintbrush to completely cover the palm and fingers of your right hand with finger paint.

3. Make a handprint on the right side of the construction paper. Make sure all your fingers, including your thumb, are straight up. Then do the same thing with your left hand, making sure that the thumbs overlap. This will create a menorah, with the overlapping thumbs being the *shammash* and the other fingers the candleholders with candles.

4. Next, cut out 16 candle flame shapes (ovals) from the yellow or orange construction paper. (You can also use white paper and color the shapes with crayons or colored markers).

5. "Light" a candle each night of Hanukkah by taping a candle "flame" above each finger/candle of your hand-y menorah.

To Spark Your Shammash...

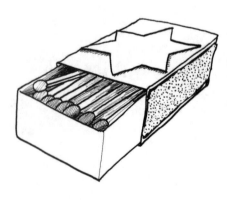

To spark your **shammash,** *you'll need matches. And won't it be nice to keep those matches in a special Hanukkah matchbox?*

What you need:

small cardboard box
silver or gold foil paper
clear tape
colored markers, crayons, or glitter glue pens
contact cement or strong glue
piece of felt
piece of sandpaper
wooden matches

What to do:

1. Simply decorate a small cardboard box (such as an old jewelry box) that is big enough to hold wooden matches inside. One nice thing to do is to cover the outside of the box with silver or gold foil, which you can buy at a craft or party store. You can also draw Hanukkah symbols on the outside of the box with colored markers, crayons, or glitter glue pens.

2. Line the bottom of the box with felt.

3. You'll need a strip of sandpaper to light the matches, so glue that to the bottom or side of the box.

4. Fill the box with wooden matches.

Now you are ready to light the menorah!

What you need:

two greeting card envelopes of the same size
white glue
scissors
ruler
colored construction paper
black marker
metallic rick rack (found in craft or sewing supply stores)

What to do:

1. Open the flaps of the envelopes. Put glue along the sides of the back of the envelopes and along the outer edges of the flaps.

2. With the backs of the envelopes facing each other, glue the flaps and sides together. This will make a dreidel shape with a pocket inside.

3. Cut a handle for the dreidel from construction paper. It should be long enough to slide all the way into the pocket to the point of the envelope, leaving a 4" handle sticking out of the other end.

4. Write your Hanukkah message on the part of the handle that will be hidden. Write PULL at the top end of the handle and slide the message part of the handle into the dreidel pocket.

5. If you used white envelopes instead of colored ones, you may want to color the dreidel with markers or crayons. Draw a Hebrew letter—*nun, gimel, hey,* or *shin*—on the front on the dreidel with a black marker.

6. Decorate the dreidel and handle by gluing strips of metallic rick rack along the top and bottom.

Envelope Dreidel Hanukkah Card

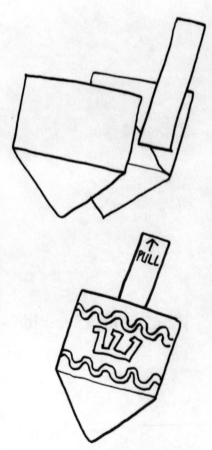

Magnetic Dreidel

What you need:

craft foam sheets in 2 colors
ruler
pen or pencil
scissors
rubber magnet
white glue
glitter glue pen

What to do:

1. Cut a piece of craft foam 2¼" wide x 2¼" long

2. Start 1¾" down one side of the craft foam and cut diagonally toward the middle. Repeat for the other side.

3. For the handle, cut a piece of the second color craft foam into a ½" x 1¼" strip and glue this strip on top of the dreidel.

4. Glue a rubber magnet (cut to size) to the back of the dreidel and let it dry.

5. Decorate your magnetic dreidel with one of the Hebrew letters drawn with a marker or glitter glue pen and then hang it on your refrigerator.

A Carton Creation

Here's an easy-to-make dreidel to give as a gift or to use in a dreidel game.

What you need:

1 empty 8 oz. cardboard milk carton
stapler
tempera paints
paint brush

colored markers
glitter glue pens (optional)
sharpened pencil

What to do:

1. Rinse out the milk carton and let it dry.

2. Fold and staple the top of the milk carton closed to create a little box.

3. Paint the box with tempera paint. You may need two coats of paint to cover the writing on the box. Allow the paint to dry completely between coats.

4. Add whatever extra decorations—glitter, sequins, etc.—you desire (for example, paint each side of your dreidel a different color, then use glitter glue to create each letter of the dreidel or draw the Hebrew letters with colored markers.)

5. Poke the pencil carefully through the bottom of the carton so that the pencil point sticks out the other side to make the point of the dreidel and the top portion of the pencil becomes the handle. Now you are ready to spin away!

Craft Stick Star of David

What you need:

6 craft sticks
blue paint or colored marker
tacky glue
silver or gold glitter glue
6" of cord or ribbon

What to do:

1. Paint craft sticks or color them with markers and let them dry.

2. Glue three of the craft sticks into a triangle. Repeat with the other three craft sticks.

3. Glue one triangle upside down on top of the other to make a Star of David. Let them dry.

4. Run a bead of glitter glue all around the star.

5. Glue a cord or ribbon in a loop to the back for a hanger or put the cord through the top triangle of the star and then knot the ends.

Metallic Star of David

What you need:

scrap cardboard or newspapers
marker
disposable aluminum pie plate
scissors
large nail
string or yarn

What to do:

1. Work on a scrap of cardboard or a thick pile of newspaper (to protect your work surface).

2. Draw a Star of David design with your marker on the pie plate and cut out the design.

3. Using a large nail (or hole punch), make a hole toward the top of one of the points of the star. This is where you will put the string for hanging your decoration.

4. Using a nail, make indentations to decorate the cut-out. You can make random indentations, regular patterns that follow the shape of the star, or a combination of both.

5. Place the string or yarn through the hole at the top of the star and hang it anywhere you like.

Recipes

A Dessert Menorah

A dessert menorah
*   can't be turned down.*
It will make a smile
*   out of any frown!*

Ingredients you need:

cake or a pan of uncut brownies, preferably with icing
pretzel rods and/or Twizzlers
peanut butter
yellow and orange M&Ms or nuts

What to do:

1. For this tasty menorah treat, you'll need a flat surface to serve as the base of your menorah—use the top of a cake or a pan of uncut brownies, preferably with icing on top.

2. The candles can be arranged on your menorah base in a number of fashions—use a long pretzel rod (broken in half) or a Twizzler (cut in half) for each candle. Using little dabs of peanut butter, attach the yellow and orange M&Ms for the flames on the flat ends of the pretzel rods or Twizzlers (or go nuts and use … nuts).

You've just created a pretty picture and a mouthwatering dessert!

A Fruity Menorah

Fruit on Hanukkah
*   makes the holiday great!*
But who needs fruit salad
*   with this on your plate?*

Ingredients you need:

28 or 29 grapes or cherries
9 pieces of pineapple or cantaloupe
1 or 2 bananas or a piece of melon with seeds removed (honeydew or cantaloupe)

Materials you will use:

9 small wooden skewers (like those used for kabobs)

What to do:

1. Use 8 skewers to spear 3 grapes or cherries apiece, and 1 skewer to spear 4 or 5 grapes. Leave the bottom half of each skewer empty to place into the base of your menorah.

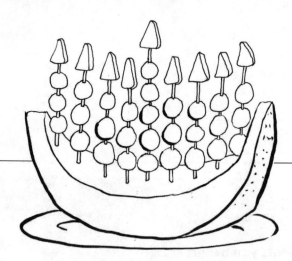

2. Now spear a piece of pineapple (or cantaloupe) at the top of each kabob. You have just made the 8 Hanukkah candles and their *shammash*, complete with flames!

3. Every menorah has a base, so place all 9 skewers (flame end up, of course) in a row into a long piece of fruit on a serving plate. For the base, try a banana or 2, or a piece of melon such as honeydew or cantaloupe—either of these will give your menorah a nicely curved base (if you use 2 bananas, see what a circular menorah looks like). You could also try using a section of pineapple.

A Dreidel Delicacy

Now you can combine the two greatest joys of Hanukkah—dreidels and food—into one fun activity! All you need are a few large marshmallows, small pretzel sticks, some peanut butter, and Hershey's Kisses.

Make your own edible dreidel by gently pushing a short pretzel stick into the marshmallow, making sure the pretzel doesn't come out the other side. Then use peanut butter to attach a Hershey's Kiss to the nonpretzel end of the marshmallow.

If you'd like to draw on the letters of the dreidel—*nun, gimel, hey, shin*—use icing from a decorator squeeze tube. You can also substitute licorice sticks or toothpicks for the pretzels.

However you decide to make your dreidel, you are just minutes away from a delicious craft for you and your friends. You may not be able to spin the dreidel, but it will surely twirl your taste buds!

Ingredients you need:

butter and flour for preparing the pan
2 cups all-purpose flour
2 cups sugar
1 cup water
$^3/_4$ cup sour cream
$^1/_4$ cup butter
$1^1/_4$ tsp. baking soda
1 tsp. vanilla extract
$^1/_2$ tsp. baking powder
2 eggs
4 oz. unsweetened chocolate, melted and then cooled to lukewarm
frosting (bought ready to spread)

Materials you will use:

12" x 8" cake pan
large bowl
mixing spoon
electric mixer (optional)
rubber spatula
toothpicks
knife for cutting
knife for icing or small metal spatula
baking sheet or large cake dish

Dreidel Cake

*Watch the dreidel
  spin, spin, spin.
Eat this cake and
  you're sure to win!*

This recipe involves sharp knives and a hot pan.

Ask an adult for help.

What to do:

1. Preheat oven to 350° F.

2. Butter and flour cake pan.

3. Mix all of the ingredients in a large bowl and beat for 5 minutes by hand or with an electric mixer.

4. Pour the mixture into the pan.

5. Bake at 350° F. for 1 hour, or until a clean toothpick inserted in the center comes out clean. Then remove the cake from the oven and let it cool in its pan.

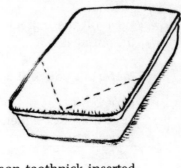

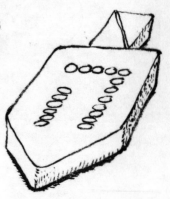

6. Cut the cake while in the pan according to the diagram, then remove the pieces to a baking sheet or a large cake dish with a metal spatula to form the dreidel.

7. Now cover your Dreidel Cake with a frosting of your choice. Frost both the top and the sides, making sure all the seams have been hidden. If you'd like, decorate the cake with small pieces of chocolate gelt (wrapped or unwrapped). Or spell out your favorite letter of the dreidel in chocolate chips or sprinkles on the top.

Serves 10–12

Note: You can take a shortcut and use a boxed cake mix instead for your Dreidel Cake.

Potato Latkes

A tasty treat for your family and friends.
Make them all year and the fun never ends!

This recipe involves hot oil that can splatter and burn.

Ask an adult for help.

Ingredients you need:

4 large potatoes, peeled
vinegar or lemon juice
3 tbsp. matzah meal
3 eggs, beaten
1 tsp. salt
$\frac{1}{4}$ tsp. pepper
1 tsp. onion powder
oil

Have all the ingredients ready for immediate use before grating the potatoes.

Materials you will use:

large bowl
large non-stick skillet
pancake turner
grater
paper towels
wooden mixing spoon
cookie sheet and aluminum foil (if the latkes are prepared ahead of time)

Fast Food Facts: Latkes

Why do we eat latkes every year at Hanukkah? No one really knows, but there are legends to help us explain the connection between this wonderful treat and the holiday. Although the most common ingredient in latkes is potatoes, eating latkes on Hanukkah may have originated from the custom of eating cheese delicacies on this holiday, which was done to honor the heroine Judith (see the story "Judith" on page 20). Most likely, Jews switched to potatoes in the Middle Ages because they were more plentiful than cheese. Another legend explains that Judah Maccabee and his soldiers hastily ate latkes on the way to a major battle with the Syrians.

What to do:

1. Grate potatoes into a bowl or pan of cold water with a few drops of vinegar or lemon juice (to prevent them from darkening), and then drain them. Using your hands, squeeze out as much water from the grated potatoes as possible.

2. Mix the grated potatoes, matzah meal, eggs, salt, pepper, and onion powder in a bowl until all is well blended.

3. Pour enough oil in the skillet so that it is $\frac{1}{4}$" deep. Heat the oil and then add a tablespoon or two of batter. When the batter starts to bubble and sizzle, add four more pancakes to the hot oil until it just begins to smoke. Flatten each slightly with the back of a spoon or a pancake turner. Fry on one side until brown, then flip over and brown the other side.

4. Remove the latkes from the skillet and drain them on paper towels.

5. Cook any remaining latke batter in the same manner, adding more oil to the skillet as needed and allowing it to get hot before adding more latkes.

Serve hot with your favorite latke toppings (such as sour cream and apple sauce).
Makes 12 latkes

Note: Potato latkes can be cooked ahead of time. Fry them in advance and allow them to cool. Then wrap the latkes in aluminum foil and freeze them. Before serving, lay the frozen latkes in a single layer on a foil-lined cookie sheet and reheat in a 375° F. oven for about 20 minutes.

Cheese Latkes

*You can eat these pancakes for dinner,
breakfast, or lunch.
They're great as a meal
or a snack to munch!*

This recipe
involves hot oil that
can splatter and burn.

Ask an adult
for help.

Ingredients you need:

1 cup small curd cottage cheese
2 large eggs, separated
$1\frac{1}{2}$ tsp. cornstarch
$\frac{1}{2}$ tsp. sugar
$\frac{1}{4}$ tsp. salt
$\frac{1}{2}$ tsp. vanilla extract
oil, about a cup or more

Materials you will use:

large bowl
large nonstick skillet
pancake turner
paper towels
electric hand mixer

What to do:

1. Mix the cottage cheese, egg yolks, cornstarch, sugar, salt, and vanilla extract in a large bowl.

2. In a separate bowl, beat the egg whites with an electric mixer until they are stiff and fold them into the cottage cheese mixture.

3. Pour enough oil in the skillet so that it is $\frac{1}{4}$" deep. Heat the oil and then add a tablespoon of batter. When the batter starts to bubble and sizzle, drop about 1 tablespoonful of the mixture into the skillet for each latke (cook about 5 latkes at a time).

4. Cook the latkes on one side until puffed and dry, then turn them with a pancake turner and brown them lightly on the other side.

5. Remove the latkes from the skillet and drain them on paper towels.

6. Cook any remaining latke batter in the same manner, adding more oil to the skillet as needed and allowing it to get hot before adding more latkes.

Serve hot with applesauce, fresh fruit, sour cream, or jelly.
Makes 36 small latkes

Ingredients you need:

2 peeled zucchini (1 pound)
1 tsp. kosher salt
1 potato, peeled
water with vinegar or lemon juice (optional)
1 tbsp. chopped fresh or 1 tsp. dried parsley
2 tbsp. all-purpose flour
salt and pepper to taste
1 large egg, beaten
2 tbsp. oil
2 tbsp. butter

Materials you will use:

colander
kitchen towel
large bowl
grater
large non-stick skillet
spatula
paper towels
cookie sheet and aluminum foil (if cooking ahead of time)

What to do:

1. Coarsely grate or shred the zucchini and place in a colander. Sprinkle the grated zucchini with kosher salt, and let it drain for 30 minutes.

2. Rinse and drain the zucchini well, squeezing out as much liquid as possible in a kitchen towel. Pat the zucchini dry again with a paper towel and place it in a large bowl.

3. Coarsely grate the potato, working quickly so that it doesn't turn brown. Or grate it into a bowl or pan of cold water with a few drops of vinegar or lemon juice (to prevent it from darkening), and then drain the gratings. Then, using your hands, squeeze out as much water from the grated potato as possible.

Green Latkes

Not sure you like zucchini?
Just try it again.
These latkes are so good,
you'll want to eat ten!

This recipe
involves hot oil that
can splatter and burn.

Ask an adult
for help.

4. Add the potato to the zucchini and then toss the mixture together with the parsley, flour, salt, and pepper. Add the egg and combine well.

5. Heat 1 tablespoon each of the oil and butter in a large non-stick skillet over medium-high heat until slightly foamy.

6. Then drop about 1 tablespoonful of the mixture into the skillet for each latke (cook about 5 latkes at a time). Flatten each slightly with the back of a spoon or a pancake turner.

7. Cook the latkes until golden, 3 minutes per side.

8. Remove the latkes from the skillet and drain them on paper towels.

9. Cook any remaining latke batter in the same manner, adding more oil and butter to the skillet as needed and allowing it to get hot before adding more latkes.

Serve hot with your favorite latke toppings.
Makes about 25 latkes

Note: Green latkes can be cooked ahead of time. Fry them in advance and allow them to cool. Then wrap the latkes in aluminum foil and freeze them. Before serving, lay the frozen latkes in a single layer on a foil-lined cookie sheet and reheat in a 375° F. oven for about 20 minutes.

Orange Latkes

Whether orange is your favorite color or not,
Come grab these yummy latkes while they're hot!

Ingredients you need:

6 carrots ($^3/_4$ lb.), peeled
1 potato, peeled
3 tbsp. fresh chives, chopped
1 tbsp. grated fresh or 1 tsp. dried ginger
2 tsp. finely grated orange peel
2 tbsp. all-purpose flour
$^1/_2$ tsp. salt and $^1/_2$ tsp. pepper or to taste
1 large egg, beaten
3 tbsp. oil
3 tbsp. butter

Materials you will use:

large bowl
large non-stick skillet
pancake turner
grater
paper towels
baking sheet and aluminum foil (if cooking ahead of time)

This recipe involves hot oil that can splatter and burn.

Ask an adult for help.

What to do:

1. Coarsely grate or shred the carrots in a large bowl.

2. Coarsely grate the potato, working quickly so that it doesn't turn brown. Or grate it into a bowl or pan of cold water with a few drops of vinegar or lemon juice (to prevent it from darkening), and then drain the bowl or pan. Then, using your hands, squeeze out as much water from the grated potatoes as possible.

3. Add the potato to the carrots.

4. Toss the mixture together with the chives, ginger, and orange peel. Sprinkle with the four, salt, and pepper, and mix. Add the egg and combine well.

5. Heat 1 tablespoon each of the oil and the butter in a large non-stick skillet over medium-high heat until slightly foamy.

6. Then drop about 1 tablespoonful of the mixture into the skillet for each latke (cook about 5 latkes at a time). Flatten each slightly with the back of a spoon or a pancake turner.

7. Cook until golden, 3 minutes per side.

8. Remove the latkes from the skillet and drain them on paper towels.

9. Cook any remaining latke batter in the same manner, adding more oil and butter to the skillet as needed and allowing it to get hot before adding more latkes.

Serve hot with your favorite latke toppings.
Makes about 30 latkes

Note: Orange latkes can be cooked ahead of time. Fry them in advance and allow them to cool. Then wrap the latkes in aluminum foil and freeze them. Before serving, lay the frozen latkes in a single layer on a foil-lined cookie sheet and reheat in a 375° F. oven for about 20 minutes.

Sweet Potato Latkes

Another orange latke,
what a surprise!
They're sweet like candy,
you won't believe your eyes.

This recipe involves hot oil that can splatter and burn. Ask an adult for help.

Ingredients you need:

1 large sweet potato, peeled
$1/2$ tsp. lemon juice
2 tbsp. matzah meal or
    whole wheat flour
2 eggs, beaten
$1/2$ tsp. salt
$1/8$ tsp. pepper, black or white
pinch baking soda
oil

Materials you will use:

Large bowl
large non-stick skillet
pancake turner
grater or food processor
paper towels
wooden mixing spoon
cookie sheet and aluminum foil (if the latkes are prepared ahead of time)

What to do:

1. Grate potato into a bowl and mix in the lemon juice to prevent browning. For a smoother texture, chop the grated potato in a food processor.

2. Mix the potato, matzah meal or flour, eggs, baking soda, salt, and pepper in a bowl until all is well blended.

3. Pour oil in the skillet. Heat the oil and then add a tablespoon of batter. When the batter starts to bubble and sizzle, add four more pancakes to the hot oil. Flatten each out slightly with

the back of a spoon or a pancake turner. Fry on one side until brown (about 5 minutes), then flip over and brown the other side. These latkes sometimes have difficulty staying together, so be careful when you turn them.

4. Remove the latkes from the skillet and drain them on paper towels.

5. Cook any remaining latke batter in the same manner, adding more oil to the skillet as needed and allowing it to get hot before adding more latkes.

Serve hot with your favorite latke toppings.
Makes 10 latkes

Note: Sweet potato latkes can be cooked ahead of time. Fry them in advance and allow them to cool. Then wrap the latkes in aluminum foil and freeze them. Before serving, lay the frozen latkes in a single layer on a foil-lined cookie sheet and reheat in a 375° F. oven for about 20 minutes.

Red Latkes

Hanukkah gelt may be gold,
but these treats are red.
So put down the chocolate
and choose a latke instead!

Ingredients you need:

1 lb. beets, peeled
$\frac{1}{2}$ lb. potatoes, peeled
1 large egg, lightly beaten
2 tbsp. all-purpose flour
1 tbsp. horseradish
1 tsp. salt
$\frac{1}{2}$ tsp. pepper or to taste
3 tbsp. oil
3 tbsp. butter

Materials you will use:

large bowl
large non-stick skillet
grater
pancake turner
paper towels
baking sheet and aluminum foil (if cooking ahead of time)

What to do:

1. Grate the beets and potatoes in a large bowl.

2. Add the egg and mix well.

3. Add the flour to the mixture and toss to combine. Stir in the horseradish, salt and pepper.

4. Heat 1 tablespoon each of the oil and the butter in a large non-stick skillet over medium-high heat until slightly foamy.

5. Then drop about 1 tablespoonful of the mixture into the skillet for each latke (cook about 5 latkes at a time). Flatten each slightly with the back of a spoon or a pancake turner.

6. Cook until golden, 3 minutes per side.

7. Remove the latkes from the skillet and drain them on paper towels.

8. Cook any remaining latke batter in the same manner, adding more oil and butter to the skillet as needed and allowing it to get hot before adding more latkes.

Serve hot with your favorite latke toppings.
Makes about 30 latkes

Apple Latkes

*An apple a day
keeps the doctor away,
But an apple latke will
attract the doctor!*

Ingredients you need:

2 cups all-purpose flour
$^1/_2$ tsp. salt
3 tsp. baking powder
1 egg, beaten
$^1/_2$ cup orange juice
2 cups apples (Red Delicious and McIntosh are good varieties), peeled and coarsely grated (or shredded)
oil
confectioners' sugar

Materials you will use:

large bowl
large non-stick skillet

grater
pancake turner
paper towels

What to do:

1. Combine the flour, salt, and baking powder in a large bowl.

2. Add the egg and the orange juice and beat well. The batter will be heavy.

3. Add the apples to the batter.

4. Add enough oil to the skillet so that it's ¼" deep, then heat the oil. Put a tablespoon of batter into the pan and when it starts to sizzle, drop about 1 tablespoonful of the mixture into the skillet for each latke. (Cook about 5 latkes at a time.) Flatten each slightly with the back of a spoon or a pancake turner. Cook until golden, about 3 minutes per side.

5. Remove the latkes from the skillet and drain them on paper towels.

6. Cook any remaining latke batter in the same manner, adding more oil to the skillet as needed and allowing it to get hot before adding more latkes.

Sprinkle with confectioners' sugar and serve hot.
Makes about 50 small latkes

Ingredients you need:

½ package dried yeast
1 cup warm water, about 105° F.
2 cups all-purpose flour, sifted
2 tsp. sugar
1 tsp. salt
1 egg, well beaten
oil
confectioners' sugar

Sufganiyot

Sufganiyot *are Hanukkah donuts in Israel.*
No matter where you eat them, this recipe won't fail!

Fast Food Facts: Sufganiyot

The modern Hebrew word *sufganiyah* (the singular of *sufganiyot*) comes from the Greek word *sufgan*, meaning "puffed and fried." The name for this favorite Israeli snack comes from Greece because Greek Jews have long enjoyed fried pancakes called *tiganites* and syrupy puffs of fried dough called *zvingos*. *Sufganiyot* are fried in oil to honor the Hanukkah miracle, and they are often filled to bursting with jelly. In fact, the pastries actually did burst when bakers sandwiched the jelly between two rounds of dough because the filling refused to stay put during the frying process. Now, every Israeli baker—it would be difficult to find one who did not make *sufganiyot* during Hanukkah—uses a modern injecting device to fill the doughy balls after they have been fried and before they have been rolled in sugar. This way each customer can enjoy the airy dough and the jelly, too.

Materials you will use:

bowl
kitchen towel
electric skillet
paper towels
sifter
candy thermometer that registers 85º F. at its lowest point

What to do:

This recipe involves hot oil that can splatter and burn.

Ask an adult for help.

1. Sprinkle the warm water over the yeast. Let it stand until the water is dissolved.

2. Sift the flour with sugar and salt in a bowl and add the egg.

3. Add the yeast mixture and mix well until the mixture is thoroughly blended.

4. Cover the bowl with a kitchen towel and put it in a warm place (85° F.), just a bit warmer than room temperature. Let it rise until it doubles in bulk. This could take an hour or more.

5. Place oil in the skillet to half the height of the pan and heat to 350–360° F.

6. Then drop about 1 tablespoonful of the dough into the skillet for each *sufganiyah* (cook about 5 *sufganiyot* at a time.). Fry each side until brown. Turn carefully.

7. Remove the *sufganiyot* from the skillet and drain them on paper towels.

8. Cook any remaining *sufganiyot* in the same manner, adding more oil to the skillet as needed and
allowing it to get hot before adding more *sufganiyot* batter. Keep an eye on the thermometer.

Sprinkle with confectioners' sugar or jam and serve
hot.
Makes 12–16 sufganiyot

Fried Hanukkah Puffs

If you think latkes are good,
  sample a puff.
You could eat twelve
  and it won't be enough!

This recipe involves hot oil that can splatter and burn.

Ask an adult for help.

Ingredients you need:

³/₄ cup milk
¹/₂ cup sugar
¹/₄ cup oil
2 eggs
3 tsp. baking powder
¹/₂ tsp. salt
2¹/₂ cups all-purpose flour
¹/₂ cup raisins, dates, or chopped apples
¹/₄ cup sugar mixed with ¹/₂ tsp. cinnamon

Materials you will use:

large bowl
electric mixer
electric skillet
paper towels

What to do:

1. In a large bowl, mix the milk, sugar, oil, eggs, baking powder,
   salt, and one cup of the flour with an electric mixer on low
   speed. Scrape the bowl constantly and mix only about 30 seconds, until the ingredients are combined. Increase the mixer's
   speed to medium and continue mixing for 2 minutes, scraping
   the bowl as needed.

2. Stir in the remaining flour and the fruit.

3. Add enough oil so that it is halfway up the side of the skillet. Set the temperature to 350° F. When the light goes out, the skillet is ready.

4. Very carefully drop a tablespoon of dough into the hot fat. Cook about 5 puffs at a time. As the puffs rise, turn them. Fry for about 2 minutes on each side or until golden brown.

5. Remove the puffs from the skillet with a slotted spoon. Drain the puffs on paper towels that are spread onto a baking sheet.

6. Fry any remaining puffs in the same manner.

7. With a spoon, combine the sugar and cinnamon in a soup bowl. While still warm, but not hot, the puffs can be rolled in the sugar and cinnamon mixture. Place a puff in the bowl with the sugar and cinnamon mixture and turn it using a spoon. Remove the coated puff to a serving bowl or platter.

Makes about 32 puffs

Bimuelos

*A Sephardic dish
   to delight your tummy.
Is there anything
   more yummy?*

This recipe involves hot oil that can splatter and burn.

Ask an adult for help.

Ingredients you need:
2 packages dried yeast
1¹/₃ cups warm water
1 egg, beaten
1 tbsp. oil
3 cups all-purpose flour
oil
cinnamon

Syrup:

24 oz. honey
¹/₄ cup of water

Materials you will use:

large bowl
electric skillet
paper towels
medium-sized pot

What to do:

1. In a large bowl, dissolve the yeast in half a cup of the warm water, about 105º F.

2. When dissolved, add the beaten egg and oil to the mixture.

3. Add all the flour and stir, gradually adding the remaining water.

4. When combined, cover bowl with a cloth towel. Let the dough rise in a warm, draft-free area for one hour or until double in size.

5. Fill an electric skillet half full with oil and heat to 350° F.

6. Then drop about 1 tablespoonful of the dough into the electric skillet for each *bimuelo*. (Cook about 5 *bimuelos* at a time.) As the *bimuelos* rise, turn them. Fry each side until golden brown.

7. Remove the *bimuelos* from the electric skillet and drain them on paper towels.

Fast Food Facts: Bimuelos

Bimuelos, small dough fritters found during Hanukkah in many Jewish communities throughout the world, are also commonly called *loukoumades*, which is their Greek name. (*Bimuelos* is the Judeo-Spanish, or Ladino, name, originating in Turkey.) Actually, the name of this dish varies in every country, as does its recipe, and the same is true within the United States.

Hawaiian *malasadas* are syrup-drenched pieces of deep-fried dough filled with custard or jam. French *beignets*, covered in powdered sugar, are popular in New Orleans. If you travel to the American South, you're sure to encounter hush puppies—little balls of seasoned, deep-fried cornmeal. And, of course, there is the doughnut. In the early 19th century, American poet Washington Irving named these golden-brown balls of fried dough after the nuts he thought they resembled.

Of course, most of these American treats are not eaten during Hanukkah alone, but the original *bimuelos* and their international relatives—Polish *ponchiks*, Middle Eastern *zalabia*, Indian *zenguola*, and others—are fried in oil to commemorate the miracle of the oil found in the ruined Temple.

8. Cook any remaining *bimuelos* in the same manner, adding more oil to the electric skillet as needed and allowing it to get back up to 350º F. before adding more dough.

9. While the *bimuelos* are frying, another person can make the syrup. Combine the honey and ¹/₄ cup water in a pot and bring to a boil. As soon as it starts to boil, remove the syrup from the heat. Watch carefully because it could boil over.

10. Dip the *bimuelos* in the warm honey syrup and sprinkle with the cinnamon.

Serve hot.
Makes approximately 45 bimuelos

Homemade Hanukkah Gelt

*Gelt is great
    to give and get.
But eating gelt made from scratch
    is better yet!*

*This recipe
involves hot oil that
can splatter and burn.*

*Ask an adult
for help.*

Ingredients you need:

16 oz. semisweet chocolate
and any of these optional additions:
several drops of mint flavoring
    or
finely chopped nuts
    or
dried apricots

Materials you will use:

large microwave-safe bowl
double boiler (optional)
large baking sheet
waxed paper
plastic knife (optional)
aluminum foil or store-bought silver or gold foil squares

What to do:

1. Pour the chocolate into a large microwave-safe bowl and cover it with plastic wrap or a microwave bowl lid. Then microwave on medium or 50% for 3–4 minutes and stirring every 2 minutes. This could take 8 minutes. Be careful not to

Fast Food Facts: Gelt

As one of the first expressions of independence after fighting King Antiochus IV and his Syrian army, the Jews created their own coinage. Thus began the history of gelt, which means "money" in Yiddish. However, the tradition to give gelt during the Hanukkah festivities did not begin until the Middle Ages, when children gave gelt to their teachers in appreciation for their work; it was the teachers' primary means of support. The custom eventually expanded to include giving coins to children to symbolize the importance of a Jewish education, especially Torah study.

Today, gelt is still important. Each year since 1958, during Hanukkah the Bank of Israel issues a special coin to be used as gelt. Throughout the years, the coins have honored different Jewish communities around the world by depicting their traditional menorahs. And, of course, gelt makes the perfect prize when playing dreidel!

overcook and burn the chocolate, and be aware that melting time will vary with different microwaves. Alternatively, melt chocolate in a double broiler, over simmering water, just until melted, then remove from heat.

2. Line the baking sheet with waxed paper.

3. Carefully spoon small, quarter-sized amounts of melted chocolate onto the waxed paper.

4. Refrigerate the chocolate until it has hardened.

5. With a plastic knife or other safe but sharp carving tool, etch designs into your gelt (such as dreidels, real coinlike images, and the money symbol: $). Use caution so you don't break the chocolate disks.

6. Remove the chocolate pieces from the waxed paper and neatly wrap each individual piece in small (2-inch) squares of foil, being sure to smooth the foil over the chocolate to make any designs you have made in the chocolate noticeable.

Variation: For extra flavor add mint flavoring to the melted chocolate—perfect as an after-dinner treat. Or add finely chopped nuts. Another option is to dip dried apricots in the melted chocolate and proceed as you would with the chocolate pieces. The round, flat, chocolate-covered fruit will look much like chocolate coins.
Makes 24 pieces of gelt

Songs

THE LATKE SONG

Music and lyrics by Debbie Friedman

Samba tempo   Cm

I am so mixed up that I can-not tell you,____ I'm
Ev - ery ho - li - day has foods so spe - cial,____ I'd
It's im - por - tant that I have an un - der - stand - ing____ of

Db

sit - ting in this blen - der tur - ning brown. I've
like to have that same at - ten - tion too. I
what it is that I'm sup - posed to do. You

Cm

made friends with the on - ions and the flo - ur,____ and the
do not want to spend life in this blen - der,____
see,____ there are ma - ny who are home - less,____ with no

Bb   **G**

cook is scout - ing o - il____ in town. I
won - der - ing what I'm sup - posed to do.
jobs, no clothes and ve - ry lit - tle food. It's

Cm

sit here won - dering what will 'come of me,____ I
Mat - za and char - o - set are for Pe - sach,____ chopped
so im - por - tant that we all re - mem - ber,____ that

can't be ea - ten look - ing as I do. I
li - ver_____ and chal - lah for Shab - bat.
while we have most of the things we need, we

need some - one to take me out and cook me,_____ or I'll
Blin - tzes on Sha - vu - ot are de - li - cious,_____ and ge -
must re - mem - ber those who have so lit - tle,_____ we must

real - ly end up in a roy - al stew. I am a lat - ke,_____ I'm a
fil - te fish no ho - li - day's with - out.
help them, we must be the ones to feed.

lat - ke,_____ and I am wait - ing_____ for_____ Cha - nu - kah to come. I am a

lat - ke,_____ I'm a lat - ke,_____ and I am wait - ing for Cha - nu - kah to

come.

2.
3. It's im—

Mi Y'maleil
Who Can Retell?

Allegro

Folksong

Round   I   II

Mi y'-ma-leil gvu - rot yis-ra eil o - tan mi yim - ne
Who can re-tell the things that be-fell us who can count them

hein b'-hol dor ya - kum ha-gi-bor go - eil ha - am
in ev'-ry age a he - ro or sage a - rose to our aid

sh'ma____ ba - ya-mim ha - heim baz-man ha - ze____
Hark____ in days of yore in Is - ra-el's an - cient

____ ma - ka - bi mo - shi-a u-fo - de____ uv-ya - mei-nu
land brave Ma-ca-be - us led the faith-ful band but now all Is-rael

kol am yis-ra - eil____ yit-a-heid ya - kum l'-hi-ga - eil____
must as one a - rise re - deem it-self thru deed and sac-ri - fice____

Maoz Tsur
Rock of Ages

Ma-oz Tzur II

O God, my saving stronghold, to praise you is a
  delight.
Restore my house of prayer where I will offer you
  thanks.
When you will prepare havoc for the foe who
  maligns us,
I will gratify myself with a song at the altar.

מָעוֹז צוּר יְשׁוּעָתִי לְךָ נָאֶה לְשַׁבֵּחַ
תִּכּוֹן בֵּית תְּפִלָּתִי וְשָׁם תּוֹדָה נְזַבֵּחַ
לְעֵת תָּכִין מַטְבֵּחַ מִצָּר הַמְנַבֵּחַ
אָז אֶגְמֹר בְּשִׁיר מִזְמוֹר חֲנֻכַּת הַמִּזְבֵּחַ

Hinei Ba
See the Conquering Hero

G.F. Handel
from Judah Macabeus

Moderately

Hi - nei___ ba b' - hod___ tok - fo
See___ the conqu' - ring he - ro comes

ba - ḥa - tsot - rot ho - du lo
Sound___ the trum - pets beat___ the drums

shi - ru zam - ru kol p' - du - yav
Sports___ pre - pare___ the laur - els bring

shi - rat ni - tsa - ḥon ei - lav
songs___ of tri - umph to___ him___ sing

shi - ru___ zam - ru kol___ p'du - yav
See___ the conqu' - ring he - ro comes

shi - rat ni - tsa - ḥon ei - lav
songs___ of tri - umph to___ him___ sing

L'vivot
Latkes

Folktune

I - ma as - ta l' - vi - vot ha - mot l' - vi -
vot ha - mot um'-tu - kot l' - vi - vot ha - mot um - tu - kot yod' -
im a - tem lih - vod ma yod' im a - tem lih - vod ma yod' -
im a - tem lih - vod __ ma lih - vod ha - ha - nu - ka

Mother made me warm latkes,
Warm and sweet latkes,
Warm and sweet latkes.
Do you know why?
Do you know why?
Do you know why?
To celebrate Hanukkah.

I Have a Little Dreydl

Allegretto

S. E. Goldfarb

I have a lit -tle drey -dl   I   made it   out of clay   and

when it's dry and read - y   then   drey - dl   I   will   play   O

drey - dl· drey - dl drey - dl   I   made   it   out of clay   o

drey - dl   drey - dl   drey - dl   now   drey - dl   I   shall play

I have a little dreydl I made it out of clay
And when it's dry and ready then dreydl I will play
O dreydl dreydl dreydl I made it out of clay
O dreydl dreydl dreydl now dreydl I shall play

It has a lovely body with leg so short and thin
And when it is all tired it drops and then I win
O dreydl dreydl dreydl with leg so short and thin
O dreydl dreydl dreydl it drops and then I win

My dreydl's always playful it loves to dance and spin
A happy game of dreydl come play now let's begin
O dreydl dreydl dreydl it loves to dance and spin
O dreydl dreydl dreydl come play now let's begin

Y'Mei Haḥanukah

Moderately

Y'-mei ha-ḥa-nu-kah ḥa-nu-kat mik-da-shei-nu b'-gil u-v'-sim-ḥah m'-mal-im et li-bei-nu lai-la va-yom s'vi-vo-nei-nu yi-sov suf-ga-ni-yot no-khal bam la-rov ha-i-ru had-li-ku nei-rot ha-nu-kah ra-bim al ha-ni-sim___ v'-al ha-nif-la-ot___ a-sher ho-l'-lu ha-ma-ka-bim

O Ḥanukah, O Ḥanukah, come light the menorah
Let's have a party we'll all dance the hora
Gather round the table we'll give you a treat
Shiny tops to play with and pancakes to eat
And while we are playing the candles are burning low
One for each night they shed a sweet light
To remind us of days long ago.

יְמֵי הַחֲנֻכָּה חֲנֻכַּת מִקְדָּשֵׁנוּ
בְּגִיל וּבְשִׂמְחָה מְמַלְאִים אֶת לִבֵּנוּ
לַיְלָה וָיוֹם סְבִיבוֹנֵנוּ יִסֹּב
סֻפְגָּנִיּוֹת נֹאכַל בָּם לָרֹב
הָאִירוּ הַדְלִיקוּ נֵרוֹת חֲנֻכָּה רַבִּים
עַל הַנִּסִּים וְעַל הַנִּפְלָאוֹת אֲשֶׁר חוֹלְלוּ הַמַּכַּבִּים

Answers

Test Your Holiday Smarts

Hanukkah Brain Teasers

(page 96-98)

What Day of Hanukkah Is It?

1) It is the third day of Hanukkah.

2) It is the eighth day of Hanukkah.

3) It is the seventh day of Hanukkah.

The Cohens

They have four children: three daughters and one son.

Four Pennies and Three Cups

Put two pennies in one cup and one penny in each of the other two cups. Then put one of the cups with one penny in it into the cup with two pennies in it. Now you have two cups with one penny in each and one cup with three pennies in it.

Hanukkah Gelt

He was given a $20 bill and a $5 bill. (One of those bills is not a $5 bill, but the other one is!)

More Hanukkah Gelt

Nathan should choose the doubling option because by doing so he can get a total of $25.50.

Even More Hanukkah Gelt

One was a $50 bill, one was a $5 bill, and three were $2 bills.

A Boatload of Mystery

One winter the van was driven to the island over the frozen lake.

Hanukkah Hugs

There were four people at the party.

Family Fun

The baker is a woman! She is the visitor's sister.

44 – 1 = 45?

This is a Roman numeral trick. The Roman numeral for 44 is XLIV. Take the "I" away (which means one) and you have XLV, the Roman numeral for 45.

Bull's-eye

3 x 17 + 49.

A Sign of Confusion

Josh knew the town they had just left. He had set the sign so that the town's name pointed to where they had been, so he knew the sign was set correctly.

The Man in Black

It is the middle of the day!

Edith's Sons

Along with their brother (he couldn't make it to the party), the three boys were triplets.

A Hot Hanukkah

Zoe lives in Australia.

Bright Brain Teasers

(page 99–100)

Spencer's Hanukkah Candles

Spencer has four candles. One is white and three are not. Similarly, one is blue, one is green, and one is yellow.

What's Wrong Here?

The Jewish calendar is lunar, based on the moon, and the first night of Hanukkah is near the end of the month when the moon is never full.

One Candle Is Carrying Holiday Weight

Take any six of the candles and weigh any three of them against the other three. If one side is heavier, then one of the candles on that side is the heavier candle. Then, take two of those and weigh them against each other. If they don't balance, you have found the heavier candle. If they do balance, the third candle is the heavier candle. If the six candles balanced, then place each of the two remaining candles on the balance and weigh them against each other to find the heavier candle.

Jacob, Jacob, Candle Maker

Yes. From the 30 sticks of wax he can make 30 candles with as many as 10 sticks of wax left over. From those 10 sticks he can make 10 candles with as many as $3\frac{1}{3}$ sticks of wax left over, from which he can make three more candles with enough wax left over to make one more. 30+10+3+1 = 44.

Tricky Wick

The wick was six feet long.

Two Candles

Thirty minutes after the candles are lit.

Three Candles

They are 6.5 inches apart.

Which Do You Light First?

The match!

Oops!

Nothing. The match needs oxygen to light. You're safe!

Selling His Way to Success?

When he started, he was a billionaire.

A Windy Night

None. It's an electric menorah.

Tasty Brain Teasers

(page 101)

Hanukkah Hunger

Sarah ate the most *sufganiyot*.

The Clever Hostess

No, because the "clever" hostess failed to give the ninth child a *sufganiyah*.

Latke, Latke

It would take five minutes, too. Just fry the latkes in the same pan!

Latkes on Schedule

Two hours. (You eat the first one right away and wait half an hour and eat the second, so in the first half an hour you have eaten two latkes.)

Fathers and Sons

The two fathers and two sons are a man, his son, and his grandson—there are only three people, but they are still two fathers and two sons.

The Large Latke

The latke weighs four pounds.

Measure Out the Oil

(page 102)

Fill the three-cup jar with oil and pour it all into the five-cup jar. Now you have three cups of oil in the five-cup jar. Next, fill the three-cup jar with oil again and pour all you can into the five-cup jar. Now you have exactly one cup left in the three-cup jar. Empty the five-cup jar. Pour the one cup that is in the three-cup jar into the five-cup jar. Then fill the three-cup jar with oil and pour that into the five-cup jar. Now you have exactly four cups of oil in the five-cup jar.

Test Your Hanukkah Thinking Skills

(page 102)

1. You have two—the two you took!

2. They would weigh the same—a pound is a pound.

3. He should check again with whom he's playing, because if he has a widow, that means he's dead!

4. Alone.

5. Neither. Candles burn shorter, but not longer. ("Which takes longer to burn?" would be a whole different question.)

6. There are no stairs in a one-floor house!

7. This question makes no sense. How could you have been in the race and been behind the last runner? For the second part, if you overtake the second-place runner you are now in second place—if you answered "first place" you goofed!

8. 44 candles—don't forget the shammash!

To calculate your Hanukkah test score, give yourself 18 points for each correct answer, 18 points for each incorrect answer, and three *sufganiyot* for completing the test!

Twenty Questions

(page 103)

1. H	11. I
2. A	12. E
3. O	13. S
4. K	14. L
5. P	15. N
6. B	16. R
7. F	17. M
8. D	18. J
9. Q	19. G
10. T	20. C

Mendel's Crazy Hanukkah Quiz

(page 104–105)

You'll find the answers just as crazy as the questions!

1. p
2. c
3. m
4. 7
5. h
6. z
7. t

If you answered 1 question correctly, you are one smart kid!
If you answered 2–3 questions correctly, you are incredibly intelligent!
If you answered 4–5 questions correctly, you are mind-bogglingly brilliant!
If you answered 6–7 questions correctly, you are a genius!

Hanukkah Mazes **Find a Path Through the Menorah**

(page 106)

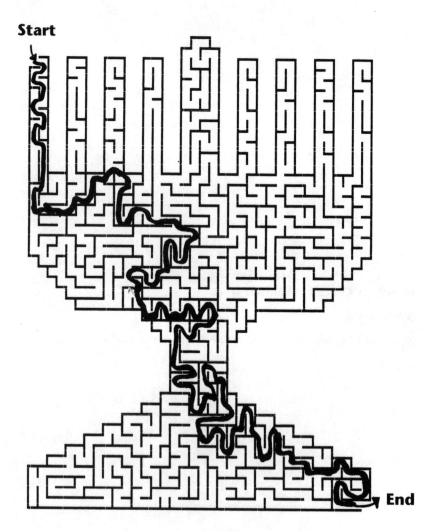

Help This Boy Light His Menorah

(page 107)

Find a Path to the Menorah

(page 108)

Start

Which Is the Candle's Wick?

(page 109)

Wick 5

Match Each Candle with Its Wick

(page 110)

Candle 1: f
Candle 2: d
Candle 3: b
Candle 4: e

Find Your Way Through the Dreidel

(page 111)

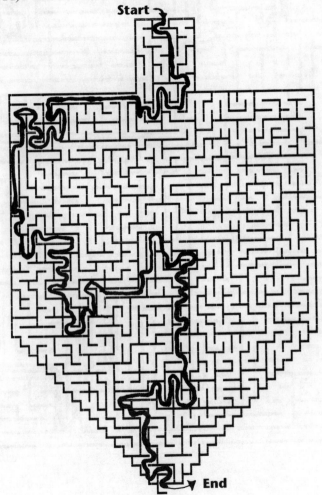

Find a Path to the Gimel

(page 112)

Find a Path to the Oil

(page 113)

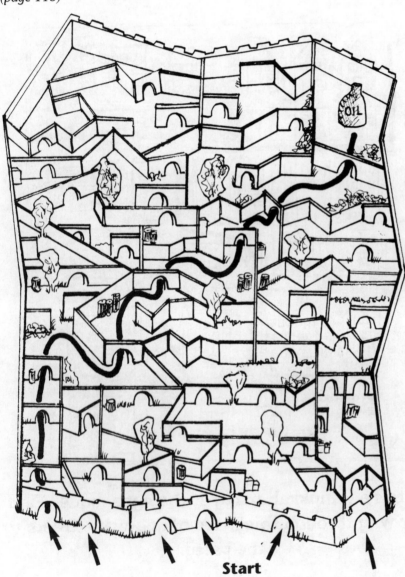

Start

Hanukkah Party at the Synagogue

(page 114)

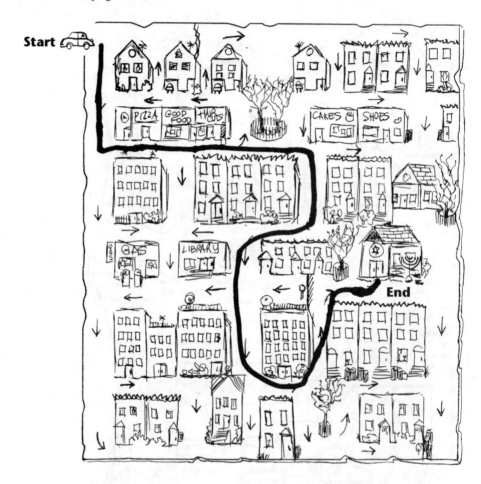

There's a Hanukkah party at the synagogue. Find your way through this maze of one-way streets to the party.

Games

Dreidel of Fortune

(page 117)

Only the Master of Ceremonies should look at the answers!

Phrase #1: People   Mattathias and his seven sons

Phrase #2: Thing   Menorah

Phrase #3: Phrase   A great miracle happened there

Phrase #4: Thing   Jug of oil

Phrase #5: Person   King Antiochus

Phrase #6: Before & After   Happy Hanukkah means dedication

Phrase #7: Things   Gelt and latkes

Phrase #8: Event   Maccabee victory

A Testy Game of Dreidel

(page 119)

The letters listed next to each number below indicate the correct statement for that question. Good luck!

1. b
2. a
3. b
4. b
5. a
6. a
7. b
8. b

Puzzle Fun

Hanukkah Number Phrases

(page 126)

1. Eight nights of Hanukkah
2. 44 candles in a box
3. Hannah and her seven sons

4. Four sides on a dreidel

5. Nine candles lit on the eight nights of Hanukkah, including the shammash

6. A menorah holds nine candles

7. Mattathias and his five sons

8. Hanukkah begins on the twenty-fifth of Kislev

Calculator Fun

(page 126)

1. Bless

2. Go

3. Giggle

4. Hello

5. Eggs

Picture Puzzles

Happy Hanukkah Rebus

(page 127–129)

It was the first night of Hanukkah. There were two menorahs by the window of Ellen's house and her parents said the blessings and lit the candles.

Ellen's father said, "We light the sandles, sing the songs, play dreidel, and eat latkes, *bimuelos*, and *sufganiyot* to remind us of the Hanukkah miracles."

Ellen's mother said, "We light the candles by the window so others will see then and remember the miracles, too."

"I must remember the Hanukkah miracles," Ellen said to herself. Ellen took a Hanukkah candle and went to her room.

Ellen gave her favorite doll Katie the candle and told her

about Hanukkah. Ellen told Katy, "If I see you holding the candle I will remember the Hanukkah miracles."

Then Ellen put her teddy bear J J near Katie. Ellen told Katie, "J J will remind me to look at you and remember the Hanukkah miracles."

Then Ellen set her toy train on the floor as if it were riding to pick up J J. "The train will remind me to look at J J and J J will remind me to look at Katie."

Ellen put a book beside the train and said, "The book will remind me to look at the train. The train will remind me to look at J J and J J will remind me to look at Katie."

Then Ellen put blocks on the floor and said, "The blocks will remind me to look at the book. The book will remind me to look at the train. The train will remind me to look at J J and J J will remind me to look at Katie."

Ellen's parents came in to her room. They saw the blocks, the book, the train, J J, and Katie. Ellen's dad asked, "Why are all these toys on the floor?"

Ellen looked at Katie, J J, the train, the book, and the blocks. "I forgot," Ellen said. "I forgot what I wanted to remember."

A Very Short Hanukkah Story

(page 130)

Once upon a time I won at dreidel but all I won were some pennies and a piece of strawberry shortcake.

Do You Know Who These Are?

(page 131)

1. MARKABEES

2. A round of dreidel

3. Candles (Canned dels)

4. The sign says, "Hanukkah is over tonight," so it is the last night of Hanukkah

What's Written or Pictured in Each Box? #1
(page 132)

1. Broken candles

2. An aerial view of a dreidel

3. Hanukkah is over Tuesday

4. You are to light on time

5. Candies and Dr. Pepper

6. At dreidel, you win some, you lose some

7. A waxless candle

8. A fancy menorah

What's Written or Pictured in Each Box? #2
(page 133)

1. The enemy was beaten

2. Two latkes on my plate

3. We light for eight days

4. The Greek armies gave up

5. There are four sides to a dreidel

6. Mattathias and his five sons

7. Light up the menorah

What's Written or Pictured in Each Box? #3
(page 134)

1. I have a little dreidel

2. The joke is on you

3. Candles in the window

4. High priest

5. The hills of Modin

6. A small bit of oil burned and burned

The Hanukkah Party
(page 135)

1. Latkes

2. 7-Up

3. Eggs sunny-side up

4. Tuna fish

5. Candies

6. Lemonade

7. Scrambled eggs

8. Leftover kugel

Peculiar Sentences
(page 136)

1. Each of the two-letter words (OH, MA, ME, IN, OR, PA, and OK) is a postal abbreviation for a state in the United States.

2. In the sentence, the word "to" is repeated.

3. The first word in the sentence is one letter, the second is two letters, the third is three, and so on.

The Candle Box

(page 137)

```
C A N D L E M C R C A N D L E L A T K E S R
B R H M O I G A H O U S E E L D N A C M E E
N C S E V E N N F O U R L C R S P C V Q U L
M O A B C O I D O N Y D U A X R O E B P E D
O G H N O A M L N R N O P N R T G L K F O N
E I Y R D M N E G A H J K D W N O D O P B A
L K U Y R L O D C G H U O L H J C N P N S C
D P O T G N E P L K S Q V E O H R A L I T E
N C A N D L E H I E C A N D L E M C U R W I
A M O I U I C A N D L E U C A N D L E J E K
C Y C A N D L E G C U E L D N A C K I O L P
B M E N O R A H I A S H A M A S H B N Y D U
C A N D L E B G T N P R C A N D L E H P N P
U R E L D N A C K D C A N D L E K F S Q A C
C A N D L E B U C L P T Y S E Y F O R Z C A
C A N D L E H Y A E P H F L G C A N D L E N
X K I Y T R U T N R F S D O C N C T Z K H D
C C A N D L E H D M R N T A Y O U A B V X L
A C A N D L E B L R A H N J H G F S N L K E
N G C D W R T R E C O D M E N O R A H D O W
D G B A B R F E D S L E L D N A C O N E L I
L T R O N P O U R E M B V F C A N D L E H E
E F O U R D H K C A N D L E B V C F Y T R S
C A N D L E L C A N D L E M E L D N A C O U
C A N D L E F E C A N D L E M O E L D N A C
```

How Many Candles?

(page 138)

There are 275 candles.

How Many Dreidels?

(page 139)

There are 50 dreidels.

Hanukkah Oddities

(page 141)

Look closely at the bottom of the menorah. What began as six bases for candle holders became nine at the top of the menorah.

Hanukkah Hijinks

Additional Hanukkah Holiday Books

prepared by Linda Silver

Younger Readers

Hart-Snowbell, Sarah. *Yesterday's Santa and the Chanukah Miracle*. Illus. by Patty Gallinger. Toronto: Napoleon Publishing, 2002, 32pp, paperback. Meeting one another by accident at the mall during the Christmas season, Annie and her grandfather's friend, Simon Greenbaum, promise not to reveal one another's Hanukkah secrets.

Hoyt-Goldsmith, Diane. *Celebrating Hanukkah*. Photographs by Lawrence Migdale. New York: Holiday House, 1996, 31pp. Learn about the symbols and customs of Hanukkah from Leora, an 11 year old who is shown celebrating the holiday with her family in many color photographs.

Jaffe, Nina. *In the Month of Kislev*. Illus. by Louise August. New York: Viking, 1992, 32pp. Rich but stingy Feivel wants to charge poor Mendel's children just for smelling his latkes. The wise rabbi teaches Feivel a lesson in giving that makes him a happier and more generous person.

Kimmel, Eric A. *The Chanukah Guest*. Illus. by Giora Carmi. New York: Holiday House, 1990, 32pp. Old Bubba Brayna doesn't see or hear as well as she used to, so when she welcomes her Hanukkah guest it isn't the rabbi but a hungry bear instead! A laugh-aloud funny story. A Sydney Taylor Book Award winner.

Kimmel, Eric A. *Hershel and the Hanukkah Goblins*. Illus. by Trina Schart Hyman. New York: Holiday House, 1989, 32pp. Alone in a haunted synagogue during Hanukkah, Hershel of Ostropol tricks seven scary goblins but on the eighth night he has to overcome their terrifying king in order to bring Hanukkah back to the village.

Kimmel, Eric A. *When Mindy Saved Hanukkah*. Illus. by Barbara McClintock. New York: Scholastic, 1998, 32pp. A family of little people who live behind the walls of New York's historic Eldridge Street Synagogue have to battle a ferocious cat named Antiochus before they can light the Hanukkah lights. Mindy and Grandpa use their wits and their courage, just like the Maccabees.

Kimmel, Eric A. *Zigazak! A Magical Hanukkah Night*. Illus. by Jon Goodell. New York: Doubleday, 2001, 32pp. A comical pair of goblins descends on the town of Brisk on the first night of Hanukkah, making mischief and scaring the townspeople until the rabbi intervenes.

Kuskin, Karla. *A Great Miracle Happened There*. Illus. by Robert Andrew Parker. New York: Willa Perlman Books, 1993, 32pp. On the first night of Hanukkah, a mother tells her family and a guest about the meaning of the Hebrew letters *nun, gimel, heh,* and *shin* on the dreidel.

Levine, Arthur. *All the Lights in the Night*. Illus. by James Ransome. New York: Tambourine Books, 1991, 32pp. Two young brothers travel on their

own from their home in Russia to a new and better life in Palestine. During the dangerous journey, a small, dented brass lamp that their mother has given them upholds their courage and their spirits.

Melmed, Laura Fox. *Moishe's Miracle*. Illus. by David Slonim. New York: HarperCollins, 2000, 32pp. Kindly Moishe wants to feed the whole village with the latkes from his magic frying pan, but his selfish wife, Baila, has other ideas. She changes her ways when little demons start popping out of the magic pan!

Schuman, Burt E. *Chanukah on the Prairie*. Illus. by Rosalind Charney Kaye. New York: UAHC Press, 2002, 32pp. Jews in Grand Forks, North Dakota? Based on true events, this is the story of an immigrant family that leaves the hardships of a small village in Galicia to make a better life on the American prairie.

Schur, Maxine Rose. *The Peddler's Gift*. Illus. by Kimberly Bulcken Root. New York: Dial, 1999, 32pp. After Leibush steals a dreidel from Shnook the peddler, he is overcome with guilt and returns it, discovering as he does so that Shnook is not the simpleton that he appears to be. A Sydney Taylor Book Award winner.

Schnur, Steven. *The Tie Man's Miracle*. Illus. by Stephen T. Johnson. New York: Morrow, 1995, 32pp. On the eighth night of Hanukkah, as Seth's family is just about to light the last candle, an old man selling ties comes to the door. Joining the family in their celebration, Mr. Hoffman tells them a story that affirms the meaning of miracles.

Spinner, Stephanie. *It's a Miracle! A Hanukkah Storybook*. Illus. by Jill McElmurry. New York: Anne Schwartz/Atheneum, 2003, 48pp. The stories that Grandma Karen tells Owen at bedtime on each night of Hanukkah are all about the miracles in his own family.

Stillerman, Marci. *Nine Spoons*. Illus. by Pesach Gerber. New York: Hachai, 1998, 32pp. During a happy family Hanukkah celebration, Grandma tells the inspiring story of a group of women in a concentration camp barracks who made a Hanukkah menorah out of spoons so that the children among them could observe the holiday. A Sydney Taylor Book Award Winner.

Older Readers

Bastrya, Judy and Ward, Catherine. *Hanukkah Fun: Great Things to Make and Do*. Boston: Kingfisher, 2003, 32pp, paperback. Learn how to make a hanukkiah, candles, dreidels, a helmet and shield, gifts to give, and more from the clear directions and bright pictures in this activity book.

Benderly, Beryl Lieff. *Jason's Miracle*. Morton Grove, IL: Albert Whitman, 2000, 120pp. A mysterious visitor takes Jason with him back into the time of the Maccabees, where they join the battle for religious freedom and see the miracle of the burning oil.

Chaikin, Miriam. *Alexandra's Scroll: The Story of the First Hanukkah*. Illus. by Stephen Fieser. New York: Henry Holt, 2002, 128pp. Readers get a vivid feel for life in ancient Israel during the Maccabean revolt from the personal news reports of Alexandra, a girl who aspires to be a scribe.

Cohn, Janice. *The Christmas Menorahs: How a Town Fought Hate*. Illus. by Bill Farnsworth. Morton Grove, IL: Albert Whitman, 1996, 40pp. Find out what happened when good people of all faiths joined together in Billings, Montana to fight hate crimes. Based on a true event.

Goldin, Barbara Diamond. *While the Candles Burn: Eight Stories for Hanukkah*. Illus. by Elaine Greenstein. New York: Viking, 1996, 60pp. Faith, traditions, religious commitment, peace, honoring women, charity, and rededication are the themes of these stories. Most are folktales but one is set in modern Israel and another is about a Holocaust survivor.

Hesse, Karen. *The Stone Lamp*. Illus. by Brian Pinkney. New York: Hyperion, 2003, 36pp. Eight poignant story poems and dramatic illustrations show how the light of the Jewish people has continued to shine, despite adversity, throughout history.

Kimmel, Eric A. *A Hanukkah Treasury*. Illus. by Emily Lisker. New York: Henry Holt, 1998, 99pp. A re-telling of the Hanukkah story, selections from the First Book of Maccabees, the history of the menorah and hannukiah, the origins of the dreidel, holiday foods from many communities, music, poetry, and ritual are all found here.

Kimmel, Eric A. *The Jar of Fools: Eight Hanukkah Stories from Chelm*. Illus. by Mordicai Gerstein. New York: Holiday House, 2000, 56pp. Wonderful stories from the famous town of Chelm, the legendary home of fools. Motke Fool, Simon Goose, Berel Dunce, and Feivel Bonehead show us how the wisdom of fools may be the wisest kind of all!

Koss, Amy. *How I Saved Hanukkah*. Illus. by Diane de Groat. New York: Dial, 1998, 96pp. Marla is the only Jew in her fourth grade class. After she decides to learn more about Hanukkah's history, meaning, and traditions, she fills her family with the Hanukkah spirit.

Penn, Malka. *The Hanukkah Ghosts*. New York: Holiday House, 1995, 80pp. Ghosts from the past add adventure and mystery to Susan's visit with her great-aunt during Hanukkah. An old house set amidst the English moors holds secrets waiting to be discovered.

Pushker, Gloria. *Toby Belfer Never Had a Christmas Tree*. Illus. by Judith Hierstein. Gretna, LA: Pelican, 1991, 32pp. Toby's family is the only Jewish one in town! She gives a party to explain the holiday to her Christian friends, including the story of the Maccabees and how to play dreidel.

Rocklin, Joanne. *The Very Best Hanukkah Gift*. Illus. by Catherine O'Neil. New York: Delacorte, 1999, 128pp. Daniel has a problem. He's afraid of dogs and a neighbor with a dog has just moved in. Find out how his problem is solved during Hanukkah.

Schram, Peninnah and Rosman, Steven M. *Eight Tales for Eight Nights*. Northvale, NJ: Jason Aronson, 1990, 66p. Stories, songs, and Hanukkah lore from around the world are all part of a book meant for young and old to share.

Singer, Isaac B. *The Power of Light: Eight Stories for Hanukkah*. Illus. by Irene Lieblich. New York: Farrar, Straus, and Giroux, 1980, 87pp. A great story-teller captivates readers with stories—some funny, some suspenseful, some serious—that show the power of light over evil.

Zalben, Jane Breskin. *The Magic Menorah: A Modern Chanukah Tale*. Illus. by Donna Diamond. New York: Simon and Schuster, 2001, 64pp. As Stanley polishes an old hannukiah, out pops a genie who spouts Yiddish and grants wishes. Stanley gets three, plus some riddles to answer. In doing so, he learns about his ancestors and about being grateful.

Reprint Acknowledgments

The author gratefully acknowledges permission to reprint the following:

"Hanukkah: The Name" by Chaim Berger, reprinted with his kind permission.

"The Story of Hanukkah" from *A Picture Book of Hanukkah* by David A. Adler and illustrations by Linda Heller, reprinted with their kind permission.

"A Hanukkah Memory" by David A. Adler, originally published in *Hanukkah, Oh, Hanukkah* by Dell Publishing and reprinted with the kind permission of the author.

"The Hanukkah of Adam and Eve: A Talmudic Legend," "Hanukkah in 1944: A True Story by Ruth Minsky Sender," "A Hanukkah Discovery" by Muriel Geralick, "A Menorah in Tel Aviv" by Ya'Akov and illustrated by Alexa Ginsburg, "The Hanukkah Gift" by Max Robin, and "Escape by Dreidel: A Legend," all from *World Over* magazine and reprinted with the kind permission of the Board of Jewish Education, New York, NY.

"Eight Gift Ideas for Eight Nights," "How Billings, Montana Defended Hanukkah," and "To Be a Lamplighter" by Menachem Mendel Schneerson, originally published in *A Different Light: The Hanukkah Book of Celebration* by Noam Zion and Barbara Spectre, reprinted with the kind permission of the American Friends of the Shalom Hartman Institute.

"The Shammash" by Rahel Musleah, originally published as "The Gift of Light" in *Hadassah Magazine* and reprinted with the kind permission of the author.

"Miracles for a Broken Planet" ©1972 by Chaim Potok, reprinted with the kind permission of William Morris Agency, Inc. on behalf of the author.

"The Little Hanukkah Lamp" by I. L. Peretz, translated and adapted by Esther Hautzig and reprinted with the kind permission of Esther Hautzig.

"K'tonton Takes a Ride on a Runaway Dreidel" and "K'tonton Arrives" from *The Best of K'tonton* by Sadie Rose Weilerstein, reprinted with the kind permission of The Jewish Publication Society.

"Chanukah Lights" by Johanna Hurwitz, reprinted with the kind permission of the author.

"The Miracle of the Potato Latkes" by Malka Penn (© Michele Palmer) and illustrated by Avi Katz, and "A Hanukkah Visitor" by Malka Penn (© Michele Palmer), both reprinted with the kind permission of the author.

"Joy to the World" by Ellen Frankel, from *Choosing to the Chosen*, reprinted with the kind permission of KTAV Publishing Company.

"A Miracle for Marci" by Miriam Rinn, originally published in *Cricket* magazine and reprinted with the kind permission of the author.

"How Jeremy Solved the December Problem" by Lois Ruby, reprinted with the kind permission of the author.

"The Hanukkah Blizzard" by Hazel Krantz, reprinted with the kind permission of the author.

"The Hanukkah of Great-Uncle Otto" by Myron Levoy and illustrated by Donna Ruff, reprinted with the kind permission of Myron Levoy.

Illustrations from *One Night, One Hanukkah Night* by Aidel Backman, reprinted with the kind permission of The Jewish Publication Society.

"The Latke Song," from *Miracles and Wonders*, music and lyrics by Deborah Lynn Friedman, published by Sounds Write Productions, Inc. and reprinted with their kind permission.

All other music was prepared by Velvel Pasternak of Tara Publications and is printed here with his kind permission.

Index

About the Author

David A. Adler is the author of more than 175 fiction and nonfiction books for young readers, many of which have been award winners. He writes the *Cam Jansen, Young Cam Jansen,* and *Jeffrey Bones Mysteries* (Viking), the *Picture Book Biography* series (Holiday House), and the *Andy Russell Books* (Harcourt). He has also written numerous picture books, as well as math, science, and economics books. Among his more than twenty-five Jewish books are several on the Holocaust, including *The Number on My Grandfather's Arm* (UAHC Press), *A Picture Book of Anne Frank, A Hero and the Holocaust: The Story of Janusz Korczak and His Children, Child of the Warsaw Ghetto,* and *Hiding from the Nazis* (all Holiday House), *We Remember the Holocaust* (Holt), and *One Yellow Daffodil* (Harcourt). Among his other Jewish books for young readers are *The House on the Roof* (Bonim and Kar-Ben), *A Kids' Catalog of Jewish Holidays* (JPS), *A Picture Book of Jewish Holidays* (Holiday House), and *Our Golda: The Story of Golda Meir* (Viking). Mr. Adler is a former math teacher and editor. He lives in New York with his wife and family.

You can look on-line at www.DavidAAdler.com and www.CamJansen.com to learn more about David A. Adler and his books.